S0-CFN-577

THE U.S.A. —

CUSTOMS AND INSTITUTIONS

The USA

CUSTOMS AND INSTITUTIONS

A Survey of American Culture and Traditions

An Advanced Reader

Ethel & Martin Tiersky

REGENTS PUBLISHING COMPANY, INC.

Series: THE U.S.A.—

Vol. I — THE LAND AND THE PEOPLE
(Vocabulary Range — 1,200 words)

Vol. II — MEN AND HISTORY
(Vocabulary Range — 1,600 words)

Vol. III — MEN AND MACHINES
(Vocabulary Range — 2,400 words)

Vol. IV — CUSTOMS AND INSTITUTIONS
(Vocabulary Range — 3,000 words)

Illustrations by Steve Perry

Published by
Regents Publishing Company, Inc.
2 Park Avenue
New York, N.Y. 10016

Printed in the United States of America

ISBN 0-88345-243-X

Preface

Customs and Institutions is the fourth and final volume in a series of graded readers about the United States. In all four volumes, vocabulary and sentence structure are kept simple so that students of English can understand the texts more easily.

Book I, *The Land and the People,* deals with the geography of the United States and discusses the nation's territorial growth from colonial times to the present.

Book II, *Men and History,* tells the stories of twenty-three famous Americans, relating a major accomplishment or well-known historical event associated with each.

Book III, *Men and Machines,* deals with important inventors and scientists, primarily those who helped to develop American industry.

Book IV, *Customs and Institutions,* discusses many different aspects of American culture, emphasizing how various immigrant groups have helped to enrich American life.

As its title promises, *Customs and Institutions* deals primarily with customs in the U.S.A.—how Americans celebrate their holidays, what they like to eat, which forms of entertainment they prefer, what sports they enjoy playing and watching. It also deals with American institutions: social, religious, educational, and political.

In addition to describing contemporary life in the United States, *Customs and Institutions* also attempts to analyze it. Concerning some aspects of American behavior, the book deals with that penetrating question: *Why*? Why is the divorce rate so high? Why do so many American mothers work? Why is there a racial problem in the U.S.A.? Why do so many adults attend school? Why is the American worker so prosperous? These are questions that every student of American society ponders, so we have tried to answer them.

Finally, we wished to tell our readers not only about how Americans behave but also about what they believe. American philosophies of education and government; American attitudes toward religion, marriage, and family life; the American outlook on life in general; and the American Dream—all are given as much attention as this thin volume will allow.

In creating a mythical "typical American" to pin our generalizations upon, we do not mean to imply that all Americans behave the same way and share the same ideals. However, American attitudes have, to some extent, been shaped by the national heritage. The more one knows about the American experience, the better one understands the people who have experienced it. In hopes of helping readers to understand Americans better, we have somewhat fearfully ventured into the realm of the abstract.

A word about what this book is *not*. It is neither a defense of American culture nor an attack upon it. Though the text does reveal obvious strengths and weaknesses, its primary intent is to describe and analyze rather than evaluate.

Obviously, so small a book cannot be more than an

introduction to the living patterns and attitudes which are characteristic of Americans. Deep insight into the American culture requires much more extensive reading, observation, and, most important, participation in American society.

Lincolnwood, Illinois — Ethel and Martin Tiersky

Table of Contents

		Page
I	The American Character	1
II	Marriage, American Style	16
III	American Family Life	28
IV	The American Economy	42
V	Labor Day and the American Worker	53
VI	Columbus Day	64
VII	Halloween	71
VIII	Thanksgiving	77
IX	Christmas and Hanukkah	86
X	New Year's Celebrations	94
XI	Holidays Honoring Two Great Presidents	101
XII	Minor Holidays	109
XIII	Easter and Related Holidays	116
XIV	Patriotic Holidays	123
XV	The American Cuisine: What and When Americans Eat	130
XVI	Evaluating the American Diet	138
XVII	American Education: The Academic Levels	150
XVIII	American Education: Philosophy, Methods, Problems, Goals	162
XIX	Religion in American Life	173

XX	News and Entertainment Media	182
XXI	Sports for Spectators and Participants	193
XXII	Americans on Vacation	205
XXIII	A Nation of Immigrants	215
XXIV	The Black American	227
XXV	The American Indian	238
XXVI	The Constitution and the Federal System	248
XXVII	Choosing the Nation's President	257
XXVIII	Citizenship and its Responsibilities	266

I
The American Character

What is an American? What are his attitudes and values? Is there a typical American personality or outlook? Dare one generalize about 212 million people living in an area of 3,615,123 square miles?

The United States is a huge nation, the fourth largest in the world. Within its borders, there are vast regional differences in climate, geography, and historical experience. Each section of the United States is often thought to have its own customs and attitudes, and stereotypes have developed about the people of each region. For example, the New Englander is described as stern and self-reliant, the Southerner as gracious and leisurely, and the Westerner as casual and friendly.

Most regional distinctions, however, have been erased by modern transportation, communication, and mass production. From coast to coast, we find the same kinds of shopping centers, supermarkets, motels, suburban houses, and urban apartments. National advertising has created national tastes in consumer goods. Home furnishings, cars, and clothing look much the same throughout the nation.

Though some regional differences remain, most notably in cooking styles and speech patterns, the attitudes and values that Americans share are of far greater significance. The pioneering spirit of the immigrant is still an important part of the American character. Except for the slaves brought from Africa, immigrants came to America voluntarily, eagerly, in search of greater prosperity and freedom.

In the mid-nineteenth century, the pioneering spirit led American settlers to travel westward by the thousands in search of land and gold. This westward movement has never ceased. Today, Northerners and Midwesterners are attracted to the West because of good business opportunities and a mild climate. From 1950 to 1970, Los Angeles (the nation's third largest city) grew 43 percent in population, while Tucson and Phoenix (Arizona's two major cities) grew more than 400 percent!

The desire to start a new life in a new place is noticeable throughout the nation. About 40 million Americans change residences every year. The average American moves fourteen times in his lifetime, compared to five moves for the average Japanese. Because so many people move so often, even those who stay put have a steady supply of new neighbors. In the United States, one cannot go home to find one's past. The old neighborhood revisited usually looks completely different, with high-rise buildings on the old softball sandlots. Childhood friends have long since moved away.

Much of this residential shifting is local and primarily related to the need for bigger or smaller living quarters as family size changes. Some local moving is also related to neighborhood changes. When families move into higher income brackets, they often move into nicer residential areas, leaving the older, deteriorating neighborhood to poorer people. Long distance moves are often related to job opportunities. Some workers move from a city where there is little chance of employment to another city where industry is expanding. Some workers, employed by large corporations, move from one city to another because job promotion within the company requires such changes. In addition, about half of the nation's young single adults live away from their home towns because they are attending college, serving in the armed forces, or just seeking new and independent lives.

What does all this moving about do to attitudes and values? Vance Packard, one of the nation's well-known nonfiction writers, discusses the problem in his popular book *A Nation of Strangers*. He believes that the highly mobile American society leaves individuals with feelings of rootlessness, isolation, indifference to community welfare, and shallow personal relationships. He urges that efforts be made to stabilize our shifting population so that Americans can "rediscover the natural human community."

Americans who do not change residence are also on the

move—traveling by air or auto to see their own country and to visit others. The need to explore a new frontier is basic to the American character. Now that most of the nation's wilderness is settled, the frontier of outer space has become the latest challenge.

The courage to try something new has been an American characteristic since colonial times, when the nation's founding fathers started one of the greatest experiments of all times—the creation of American democracy. The citizens of the United States, through their elected representatives, establish the nation's laws and determine its foreign policy. Those who disapprove of the laws and policies established by their representatives may openly express their disapproval and try to elect new representatives to carry out their wishes.

American democracy means majority rule, but it also means protection of minority rights. There are certain freedoms which the United States promises to all its citizens, and members of minority groups cannot be denied these rights by a vote of the majority. The basic rights of every citizen, outlined in the first ten amendments to the Constitution, are known as the Bill of Rights. These rights include freedom of speech, freedom of religion, and freedom from unreasonable search and arrest.

In the United States, democracy is not only a form of government; it is a way of life. The belief that those who must live by the rules should help make the rules is basic to nearly all American institutions and organizations. American children are introduced to the democratic concepts of majority rule and representative government at a very early age. Many families hold weekly meetings to determine household rules and activities. Most schools have a student council with elected representatives so that students can voice their opinions about school regulations and activities. Social, civic, labor, and charitable groups elect their officers and vote on issues. In business, stockholders elect the directors they feel are best qualified to control the company. Local and state governments are also based upon democratic principles.

"All men are created equal," says the Declaration of Independence. This statement does not mean that all human beings are equal in ability or ambition. It means, instead, that all people should be treated equally before the law and given equal privileges and opportunities, insofar as government can control these. In practice, this ideal often does not work perfectly. There have always been those who would deny the rights of others for their own self-interest. There are times when the American people need to be reminded that *any* denial of basic rights is a weakening of the total system. However, equal treatment and equal opportunity for all are ideals toward which American society is moving ever closer.

The American belief in equality of opportunity is illustrated by the Horatio Alger myth. Horatio Alger was a nineteenth-century American novelist who wrote stories about poor boys who became successful. His books told about the little newsboy or bootblack who, because he was hardworking, honest, and lucky, grew up to become rich and respected. These popular "rags-to-riches" stories exemplified the American Dream—the belief that any individual, no matter how poor, can achieve wealth and fame through diligence and virtue.

For many immigrant Americans, this dream became reality. Most of them, particularly those who came to the United States during the nineteenth century, were peasants and laborers in their native lands. Within a generation or two, nearly all these immigrant families rose on the social and economic scales. Financial success was often the result of taking a risk, of quitting a salaried position and starting a new business. Becoming an entrepreneur is still an open, though sometimes rugged, pathway to prosperity.

Social mobility—movement from class to class—has always been characteristic of the United States. However, although sociologists talk of the country's class structure, most Americans do not think in these terms. They do not see themselves as struggling to move from the lower middle class to the upper middle class. Instead they think in terms of higher income to pay for a bigger house, a trip to Europe, summer camp for their children, or more retirement insurance.

Prior to the mid-1960s, American initiative to experiment was encouraged by a generally optimistic outlook. The typical American believed in trying something new in an attempt to make life better. He had a firm faith in the possibility, even the probability, of progress. This attitude was based upon his own and his family's past experiences. Older people often told their children about how hard life had been before the invention of countless work-saving devices and ready-made products. Parents could remember the days when orange juice had to be squeezed from oranges by hand rather than poured from a can and diluted. Grandpa could recall mowing the lawn with a manual mower. Grandma described the old-fashioned washer and feeding the clothes into the wringer, piece by piece. Great-grandma showed the blisters on her hands from churning butter and cranking the ice-cream maker. Great-grandpa talked about walking five miles to school before the days of public transportation and car pools.

Because life was getting easier, people assumed that it was getting better. The prevailing American attitude was one invented by a French pharmacist who, in treating his patients by hypnosis, instructed them to say, "Every day in every way I am getting better and better." Until the mid-1960s, the typical American had this kind of faith in automatic improvement. But by the end of the decade, this national optimism, which set the United States apart from all other nations, was gone.

Before the mid-1960s, Americans shared another happy attitude—a naive patriotism that said the United States was the best of all possible places; that American policy was determined by ethics, not expediency; that we had never fought an unjust war; that we were always on the side of right and ruled by noble motives.

Then came the 1960s, a period when Americans realized that if conditions could change for the better, they could also change for the worse. Even more frightening, people began to notice that the quality of life in the United States was already changing for the worse, and that if serious and immediate efforts were not made to stop the trend, life would soon be unlivable in this best of all possible places. Americans also realized that their government, big business, and other major institutions were not always ethical and could not always be trusted to do what would be best for the nation and the world.

What killed American optimism? First and perhaps most important, there was the Viet Nam War. During the 1960s, American involvement kept growing, and the bloodshed entered the American living room via TV. The horrors of our twelve years there—46,000 American dead and many more Vietnamese—formed only one part of the violence which characterized the decade. Several assassinations of public figures and a continued rise in the violent crime rate led to a great demand for gun control legislation. There were race riots in many cities, student riots on many campuses, policemen with tear gas and guns to quiet the rioters, and TV cameramen to bring it all home to the American public.

Public protests (both violent and nonviolent) left their mark upon the American character. Noisy demonstrations occurred as various groups pointed out that they had always been discriminated against in this country. Women, blacks, Indians, and Spanish-speaking citizens all gave their versions of American history and destroyed any remaining illusions that this nation has offered freedom, justice, and equality to all. White Americans began to feel guilty about their aggressive destruction of non-white cultures. American men were warned that the exploited, subservient American housewife was a dying breed. Women's Liberation groups deplored the "packaged" woman whose major interest was in maintaining an attractive facade in order to win and hold a husband. This type of woman was depicted as a victim of and a traitor to her sex.

In the 1960s still another exploited American made himself heard—the consumer. Choosing daily from a vast array of goods, the American shopper often found that the products he brought home were not what he assumed they were, not what they claimed to be, and sometimes not even safe to use. The idea of consumer protection received a big boost in 1962 when President Kennedy delivered a special message listing four basic consumer rights: the right to safety, the right to be informed, the right to choose, and the right to be heard. Then, in 1965, a young lawyer named Ralph Nader published a shocking book telling the American public that their automobiles were unnecessarily dangerous. As a result of his efforts, the huge automobile industry was forced to produce a safer product. Seat belts became standard equipment, designs were changed to reduce injuries from collisions, and automobiles with faulty mechanisms were recalled for repair.

Nader came upon the scene at a time when big business was giving the public a great many shoddy goods and services. His success in dealing with the auto industry inspired others to campaign for better products. Today more than a thousand consumer programs are operated by the federal government. The majority of state governments have consumer fraud units, and more than fifty cities have agencies to protect the consumer. Legislation has done much toward accomplishing the concerned consumer's two major goals—product safety and truth in advertising. Labeling on packaged foods is more explicit than ever before. Manufacturers of dangerous articles (such as cigarettes and toxic substances) must label the products with appropriate warnings. In 1973, the labeling of ingredients in cosmetic products became mandatory.

Today the American shopper is better protected against fraud and danger than ever before. In addition, people are learning to purchase more intelligently and economically. All across the country, consumer cooperatives are developing, enabling members to buy goods at wholesale prices. Also, schools, unions, supermarket chains, and many other organizations are helping to educate buyers so that they will get the most and the best for their money.

Of all the protest groups competing for public attention during the 1960s, the most alarming were those that spoke out against pollution. Americans learned that their air, water, land, and food were being polluted in a variety of ways. This pollution was reaching a dangerous level which could in the near future become a threat to human, plant, and animal life. Air pollution was coming primarily from automobile exhaust fumes and industrial smokestacks. Water pollution was due to industrial waste, garbage, detergents, and other sources. The land and its animal and plant life were being polluted by a variety of man-made chemicals, especially insecticides and herbicides. Disposable but indestructible products of plastic and metal were cluttering the land. Consumers were asked to buy only products that could be *recycled* (converted back into raw material and manufactured into usable items over and over again). Recycling centers were created for the collection of newspapers, glass bottles, aluminum cans, and other reusable items. Americans were encouraged to bring these products to the recycling centers rather than discard them with other garbage.

Ecology, which refers to the interrelationship of living things and their environments, is a word which became familiar even to children. Everyone was urged to ask himself, "What effect will my actions have upon other living things and eventually upon the quality of life itself?" Americans, who produce about 30 percent of the world's pollution, were reminded that the greatest polluters of all are people and perhaps the greatest of all threats to the environment is overpopulation. Birth control was strongly advocated, and Americans responded by having fewer children.

Out of all the negatives of the 1960s came a great deal that was positive. As Americans became fully aware of existing evils, they began to look for ways to combat them. Americans responded in a typically American way: by organizing. Throughout the nation, groups of concerned citizens banded together to exert their united influence against the forces they dreaded. There were anti-war groups, women's lib groups, population control groups, groups asserting the needs and rights of various cultural minorities, groups fighting to protect the environment from pollution, and so on. In general, these groups had two goals—first, to educate the public and thereby alter attitudes and behavior; second, to influence governmental bodies to pass legislation that would benefit their causes.

Many people described the 1960s as a decade overcome by pessimism and despair; yet during this period activists all over the nation still believed that by working together they could improve conditions. Although some activist groups were revolutionary, most were merely reformist. Their members believed that necessary changes could be brought about without overthrow of the nation's political and economic system. Many problems of the 1960s have remained with us into the seventies, but vigorous efforts to deal with them have met with some success and have given the nation new hope.

Problems of pollution and consumption are greater here than elsewhere because Americans are dependent upon a great many possessions. The United States contains only six percent of the world's population; yet this six percent makes, buys, sells, and uses more than one third of the world's goods and services. Americans produce and consume more than any other nation. Less than a century ago the average citizen had a list of seventy-one "wants." Sixteen of these were considered necessities. Today, the average American's wants have grown to 464, and only about ninety-four are considered necessities.

The American need to own things is partly the result of mass advertising, which urges consumers to discard last year's car or clothing in favor of the current models with the latest designs. Some people are convinced that they must "keep up with the Joneses," that they must have whatever their neighbors have. The old car or the old stereo set may work perfectly, but a newer and bigger one might raise the family's esteem in the community. Possessions become symbols of financial success; they elevate one's social status.

Advertisers also appeal to the American desire to look youthful and be physically attractive. Commercials attempt to sell many products—shampoo, toothpaste, deodorant, and soap, for example—by implying that their particular brand will help its user be more appealing.

But Americans also make many purchases for practical reasons. They buy labor-saving devices to do routine household chores more quickly and easily. Every housewife wants a vacuum cleaner, an electric mixer, a steam iron, an automatic clothes washer and dryer, and a dishwasher. Nearly every home-owning husband would like a power lawn mower, a snow-blower, and an electric drill.

Americans also buy things because they like to do things. Equipment for hobbies and books about "do-it-yourself" projects are very popular. Americans want to know how to cook with a "continental" flair while refinishing the bedroom furniture and making a million dollars in the stock market. The American love of activity is part of a generally pragmatic outlook on life, a belief that the value of knowledge is related to its usefulness.

Because of their tremendous expenditures for goods and services, Americans are often accused of being materialistic, of valuing above all else money and the comforts and pleasures that money can buy. However, Americans are, on the whole, quite idealistic. They ask much more of life than just day-to-day enjoyment and financial security. They ask that life be meaningful. In choosing careers, Americans consider the significance of their work just as important as the income the job will bring. Also, most Americans are still under the influence of the Protestant ethic, which considers a life of pleasure sinful and hard work ennobling. Americans place great value upon useful activity. In fact, many cannot enjoy their expanding number of leisure hours unless most of their "free" time is spent doing something constructive —such as working on the lawn or cleaning out the garage.

True, Americans enjoy money and the things it can buy. But in defense of the so-called materialistic American, one expert in American culture points out, ". . . however eager we are to make money, we are just as eager to give it away. Any world disaster finds Americans writing checks to relieve distress. Since the war we have seen the spectacle of the United States sending billions and billions of dollars' worth of goods to countries less fortunate than we. Write some of it off, if you will, to a desire to buy political sympathy; there is still an overplus of goodwill strictly and uniquely American. Generosity and materialism run side by side."

The average American is also accused of being "rough around the edges"—that is, of lacking sophistication in manners and understanding of things cultural. He tries hard to polish those edges through education and travel. But no matter how much he learns and sees, his interests are less with the past than with the present and future, less with the decorative than with the functional. He may be bored by medieval art but fascinated by modern engineering. Foreigners will find him always ready to compare cultures, though he may conclude that American methods are more efficient and therefore better. In expressing his views, he may be blunt to the point of rudeness. He admires efficiency and financial success. Eager to get as much as possible for his time and money, he is sometimes impatient, tense, and demanding. Often, he is in a hurry and unable to relax. His intensely competitive outlook is probably his greatest fault. But one must give him credit for his virtues: he is friendly, spontaneous, adaptable, efficient, energetic, and kindhearted. All things considered, he is a likable guy.

EXERCISES

Comprehension. Choose the correct answer.

1. Among the nations of the world, the United States is the
   (a) largest.
   (b) fourth largest.
   (c) second largest.
2. The American government is based on principles of
   (a) monarchy.
   (b) democracy.
   (c) anarchy.
3. Horatio Alger was a
   (a) communist.
   (b) novelist.
   (c) ecologist.
4. The statement "All men are created equal" means that all men should have equal
   (a) opportunities.
   (b) salaries.
   (c) intelligence.
5. The 1960s were years of
   (a) public apathy.
   (b) public protest.
   (c) widespread contentment.
6. The American Dream is the belief that any individual can achieve wealth and fame through
   (a) birth and privilege.
   (b) hard work and honesty.
   (c) exploitation and violence.
7. Social mobility means movement from
   (a) class to class.
   (b) city to city.
   (c) country to country.
8. Ralph Nader is
   (a) a United States senator.
   (b) a crusader for consumer rights.

(c) an automobile company executive.

9. The field of ecology is concerned with
   (a) the advertising industry.
   (b) minority rights.
   (c) the quality of the environment.

10. In the American economy, advertising plays
   (a) a major role.
   (b) a minor role.
   (c) an unimportant role.

Vocabulary and Usage. Give the meaning of each of the following words. Use each in a sentence.

character	middle class
regional	majority
value	consumer
ecology	institution
democratic	minority
entrepreneur	expediency

Conversation and Discussion. Describe the most important aspects of the American character.

II
Marriage, American Style

Love and marriage, love and marriage;
They go together like a horse and carriage.

So go the lyrics of a well-known American song. The horse and carriage is a thing of the past, but love and marriage are still with us and still closely interrelated. Most American marriages, particularly first marriages involving young couples, are the result of mutual attraction and affection rather than practical considerations.

In the United States, parents do not arrange marriages for their children. Teen-agers begin dating in high school and usually find mates through their own academic and social contacts. Though young people feel free to choose their friends from diverse groups, most choose a mate of similar background. This is due in part to parental guidance. Parents cannot select spouses for their children, but they can usually influence choices by voicing disapproval of someone they consider unsuitable.

However, marriage between members of different groups (interclass, interfaith, and interracial marriages) are increasing, probably because of the greater mobility of today's youth and the fact that they are restricted by fewer prejudices than their parents. Many young people leave their home towns to attend college, serve in the armed forces, or pursue a career in a bigger city. Once away from home and family, they are more likely to date and marry outside their own social group.

In mobile American society, interclass marriages are neither rare nor shocking. Interfaith marriages are on the rise, particularly between Protestants and Catholics. Though parents may disapprove, the general population does not censure interfaith marriages. On the other hand, interracial marriage is still very uncommon. It can be difficult for interracial couples to find a place to live, maintain friendships, and raise a family. Marriages between people of different national origin (but the same race and religion) have been commonplace here since colonial times.

The average American man is about twenty-three years old at the time of his marriage; his bride is about twenty-one. Traditionally, when a couple decides to marry, the man gives his fiancée a diamond engagement ring. When the engagement period begins, the bride-to-be and her future husband meet each other's relatives, make preparations for their wedding and honeymoon, and plan their future together.

Very few newlyweds choose to begin married life living with either set of parents. Therefore, during the engagement period, most couples look for their own apartment and buy furniture and other items for their new residence. Fortunately, the financial strain of setting up housekeeping is eased considerably by wedding gifts. Although the old-fashioned dowry (a set sum of money promised to the groom by the bride's father) is no longer customary, the bride's parents are usually expected to provide their daughter with a trousseau of clothing, linens, and some kitchen equipment. Relatives and friends send money or household appliances. They may also arrange a *shower*—a party just for women at which each guest gives the bride-to-be a gift useful for cooking or housekeeping. Two or three nights before the wedding, the groom and his close friends traditionally celebrate at an all-male party called a bachelor or *stag* party. On this occasion, the groom may receive an expensive gift purchased jointly by all the guests.

Traditionally, the bride and groom do not see each other on their wedding day until they meet at the altar, nor is the groom supposed to see the wedding dress at any time before the ceremony. Besides a white gown and veil, the bride usually wears "something old, something new, something borrowed, and something blue."

The wedding itself is usually paid for by the bride's parents, although the groom and his parents help prepare the guest list. The day's festivities begin with the marriage ceremony, which may be held in a church, synagogue, home, or hotel ballroom. In a religious ceremony, guests are seated on either side of an aisle, and the wedding starts with a procession down the aisle. The procession includes the bridal couple and their closest relatives and friends. In addition to parents and perhaps grandparents, there are usually bridesmaids and a maid of honor (all wearing matching dresses), ushers, and the groom's *best man*, who carries the wedding ring. Immediately preceding the bride, there may be a flower girl strewing the path with petals from a straw basket. The bride walks down the aisle with her father, who leads her to the altar and "gives her away." The bride and groom face the officiating clergyman as he recites the traditional ceremony. A wedding band is placed upon the bride's finger, the clergyman says, "I now pronounce you man and wife," and the newlyweds lead the recessional up the aisle. The entire ceremony seldom takes longer than forty-five minutes.

As the bridal couple leave the church, guests may throw rice, rose petals, or confetti at them. Sometimes the bridal car is decorated with paper streamers, old shoes, and a "Just Married" sign.

After the ceremony, there is usually a party where guests enjoy refreshments and dancing. During the meal, the wedding cake—a tall, many-tiered cake with a miniature bride and groom on top—is displayed. After dinner, the bride and groom cut into the cake, and it is served to the guests.

Just before the bride leaves the wedding party, she throws her bouquet to her bridesmaids. Supposedly, the girl who catches the bouquet will be the next to marry. The bride's garter may also be thrown to the single men at the wedding. Catching the garter also signifies an approaching marriage.

After the wedding, the newlyweds usually take a one- to

two-week honeymoon trip. When they return home, the bride probably continues with work or school until she is ready to have children.

Most brides follow closely the traditional wedding customs. But the charm of the traditional wedding is sometimes overshadowed by extravaganza. Every year Americans spend about $7 billion (an average of $3,600 per bride!) for goods and services related to getting married. The engagement ring alone may cost from several hundred to a few thousand dollars. Sometimes the bride's family employs a company that specializes in planning and running weddings. Engraved invitations, a fancy rented hall decorated lavishly with flowers, a professional photographer, musicians, a wedding gown that may cost a few hundred dollars, rented formal clothes for the men in the bridal procession, a good deal of liquor, an elegant dinner, a colossal wedding cake, a beautiful "sweet table"—all this may be provided for the enjoyment of 200 or more guests and may cost thousands of dollars. Parents often spend more on a daughter's marriage than on her entire education! Though the amount spent varies from one family to another, the custom of overspending on weddings is widespread at every economic level and in every religious and ethnic group.

Rebelling against the lavish excesses and incredible expense of the large American wedding, a small percentage of engaged couples choose to "do their own thing." Some reject the decorated hall and get married in an outdoor setting of natural beauty—a park, forest, beach, hilltop, or even a cave. Dress is whatever the bride and groom consider festive, but it is certainly not the traditional formal attire. Sometimes the bride and groom write part of the service themselves and exchange vows that are specifically meaningful to them. Sometimes each recites a favorite poem. The traditional promise of "till death do us part" is often replaced by "as long as our love endures" or (in popular slang) "for as long as we both dig it." In general, these nontraditional ceremonies speak not only of friendship, love, and devotion, but also of self-growth, equality, and individual rights. These services reveal that the participants are not only idealistic and optimistic about marriage, but also realistic.

Although large wedding celebrations are traditional, the engaged couple may ignore tradition and get married without fanfare. To be legally wed, they need only fulfill the requirements set by the state in which the ceremony is performed. Ordinarily, a license must be obtained. Each state prescribes who may get a license to marry. In most states, eighteen-year-olds can marry without their parents' consent. With parental consent, nearly all states will allow a marriage between a sixteen-year-old girl and an eighteen-year-old boy, and some states have even lower age limits. Marriages between first cousins or couples more closely related are prohibited in many states. Most states require medical examinations and certificates before issuing a marriage license and refuse licenses to persons with certain physical or mental illnesses. Once given a license, the couple appears before someone authorized to perform marriages (usually a judge or ordained religious leader), who marries them according to the prescribed form. Second marriages are usually small affairs with only close relatives of the bridal couple as guests.

During the traditional wedding ceremony, the bridal couple promise each other lifelong devotion; yet, nearly one out of every three American marriages ends in divorce. What goes wrong? The fact that divorces are so common in the United States does *not* mean that Americans consider marriage a casual, temporary relationship. Just the opposite is true. Americans are extremely idealistic about marriage. They desire a close and intense bond with their partners. They seek physical, emotional, and intellectual compatibility. They want to be deeply loved and deeply understood. Paradoxically, it is because Americans expect so much from marriage that so many get divorced. They prefer no marriage at all to a marriage without love. With typical American optimism, they end one marriage in hopes that the next will prove more successful.

In many homes, divorce is caused by the "battle between the sexes." To understand the problem, one must remember that the contemporary American woman is "emancipated." During childhood and adolescence, the American girl is given freedom and education equal to a boy's. After completing her schooling, she is able to get a job and support herself. She does not need to marry for financial security. She considers herself an independent, self-sufficient person and will not accept a subservient role in marriage. She wants a husband whom she can respect, but she does not want to be dominated by him. She wants a democratic household in which she has a voice in making decisions that affect the entire family. When a husband and wife are able to share decision-making, their marriage is probably closer, stronger, and more satisfying than those of past generations. When husband and wife battle for dominance, the couple is likely to wind up in the divorce courts.

When a couple gets divorced, the court usually requires the man to pay his former wife a monthly sum of money called *alimony*. The amount of alimony depends upon the husband's income, the wife's needs, and the duration of their marriage. When the couple has had children, they usually remain with the mother, and the father is expected to pay for their support. It is generally specified that the children will spend Saturdays or Sundays, some holidays, and perhaps summer vacations with the father.

Although divorce is quite common in the United States, 80 percent of those who get divorced remarry. Poking fun at the frequency of remarriage, one well-known American joke tells of a wife calling to her second husband, "Quick, John! Come here and help me! Your children and my children are beating up our children!"

Because so many Americans get divorced, and many more are unhappily married, the institution of marriage has been under vigorous attack during the last ten years. Many people seek to modify marriage or find alternatives to it. Some of the alternative patterns of living now practiced openly by growing numbers of people include: unmarried couples living together, parenthood without marriage, polygamy (which is illegal), homosexuality, and communal living. Still, marriage is by far the most popular lifestyle in the United States. The 1972 statistics revealed that of Americans eighteen years or older, 71 percent of women and 78 percent of men were married. About 95 percent of middle-aged Americans have been married at least once.

Many pressures are now at work to modify the American marriage. One of these is the Women's Liberation movement. The traditional marriage (as described by many exponents of Women's Liberation) is a trap. It forces the woman to devote herself fully to the service of others with no time left to develop her own interests or talents. She is no longer a person in her own right but someone's wife and someone's mother. She is faced with the exhausting obligations of feeding, clothing, nursing, chauffeuring, and running countless errands for her family. Then there is the housework, which is uncreative, repetitious, monotonous, and unending. All these duties convert the educated American woman into a dull and discontented person. When the children grow older and the job of homemaker becomes easier, the housewife (out of touch with the working world for several years) cannot compete with men for an interesting and meaningful job. Thus, say the leaders of Women's Liberation, a woman's intellectual and creative energy is stifled by a culture which imposes on her an unstimulating lifestyle. Of course, many housewives disagree with this argument. They find many aspects of homemaking creative, challenging, and interesting, and they are able to fill up their leisure time with volunteer work that they consider worthwhile.

In the American marriage, who is really being exploited? There are wives who work outside the home all day and then spend their evenings and weekends doing housework and grocery shopping. There are wives who take care of their pre-school children all day and do housework at night. Some of these women consider themselves overworked. However, there are also wives whose children are in school all day, who have part-time help to do the housework, and who do not need to get a job to help support the family. Some of these women enjoy a life with much leisure time; yet others feel useless and bored. While many upper-middle-class women are taking tennis lessons, playing cards, doing volunteer work, lunching with friends, and browsing in department stores, their husbands may be putting in long, hard hours at high-pressure jobs. In these households, it is often the husband who feels exploited.

Among married couples, one finds a wide range of living patterns. Probably the majority of couples are still living the traditional way, with the husband as breadwinner and the wife as homemaker. In many households, both husband and wife are happy with this arrangement. But in a recent survey, 40 percent of young wives said they would prefer to share both financial and domestic responsibilities with their husbands. And no doubt many husbands would welcome their wives' assistance in supporting the family.

About 19 million married women (approximately 42 percent of American wives) hold jobs outside the home. Most of these women work at routine jobs because their families need the income. In many households, where both parents work, husbands help with the homemaking. Thanks to Women's Liberation, rigid notions about certain tasks being "women's work" are being discarded. In recent years, many fathers have discovered that they enjoy spending more time taking care of their children and cooking for the family. Some couples have even restyled their lives so that both husband and wife work part time and share equally the responsibilities at home. No doubt this lifestyle would be practiced by many more couples if not for the difficulty of pursuing careers on a part-time basis.

Women's Liberation has also convinced many wives that child care should not be their sole life's work. The birth rate is declining, partly in response to concern about overpopulation. The number of married couples who choose to remain childless is increasing. In 1973, abortion during the early months of pregnancy became legal throughout the United States, and large numbers of women (unmarried and married) have been taking advantage of the new law. Women's Liberation groups fought long and hard for this right not to bear and raise unwanted children. These groups are now fighting for more government-supported day care centers, which would enable mothers of pre-schoolers to continue to work.

Attitudes change much faster than behavior. While many couples cannot alter their own way of life, many are teaching their children that the traditional marriage is not the only way and perhaps not the best way to live. As housewife and mother, the typical American woman does not seem to consider herself exploited. She does, however, see that there are other possibilities—that marriage is not the only lifestyle for women and that even the married woman can be something more than wife and mother.

EXERCISES

Comprehension. Choose the correct answer.

1. Most Americans find their mates through
   (a) social contact.
   (b) parents.
   (c) marriage brokers.
2. Interclass, interfaith, and interracial marriages are
   (a) decreasing.
   (b) remaining the same.
   (c) increasing.
3. The average age of a newly married woman is about
   (a) thirty.
   (b) fifteen.
   (c) twenty-one.
4. The wedding is usually paid for by the
   (a) bride and groom.
   (b) groom.
   (c) bride's parents.
5. Before a couple may be married, they must obtain
   (a) a wedding ring.
   (b) a job.
   (c) a license.
6. American marriages tend to be
   (a) dominated by the husband.
   (b) democratic.
   (c) dominated by the wife.
7. In the United States, the percentage of wives who work is about
   (a) 3 percent.
   (b) 42 percent.
   (c) 58 percent.

8. The number of American marriages that end in divorce is about
   (a) one out of three.
   (b) one out of five.
   (c) one out of seven.
9. Americans are prohibited by law from obtaining
   (a) abortions.
   (b) divorces.
   (c) two marriage partners at the same time.
10. The divorced man is usually required to pay his former wife a monthly allowance called
   (a) polygamy.
   (b) hypocrisy.
   (c) alimony.

Vocabulary and Usage. Give the meaning of each of the following words. Use each in a sentence.

mobility	procession
prejudice	honeymoon
fiancée	adolescence
trousseau	divorce
tradition	alimony
dowry	shower

Conversation and Discussion. Discuss the way Americans decide whom they will marry. Compare this with the way marriages are contracted in other countries.

III
American Family Life

In the United States, the family is still very much alive, despite its many ailments. The vast majority of Americans live with people to whom they are related by blood or marriage. There are about 53 million American families (including married couples that do not have children living with them). Most American couples have two or three children, though larger families are not unusual.

Typically, the family group that occupies one household consists of parents and their unmarried children. Middle-aged and elderly people generally do not live with their married children. However, parents usually keep in close contact with their grown children and take great interest in their grandchildren. On holidays, members of the larger family group—grandparents, aunts, uncles, and cousins—often dine together.

About three-fourths of American families live in areas classified as urban, though this label includes many different styles of living. Less than five percent of Americans live on farms, but small town living is still widespread. About 50 million Americans live in communities smaller than twenty-five hundred. The United States has more than a thousand cities with populations between ten and twenty-five thousand. However, more than two-thirds of Americans live in or near cities of fifty thousand or more. A greater number of Americans live in suburbs (about 37 percent of the population) than in cities (about 31 percent).

Each type of community has its virtues and its limitations. Intimate, slow-paced rural and small town living often seems dull and stifling, especially to young, single people. Suburbs offer the advantages of small town living with the facilities of the big city nearby. But suburban living is often criticized for its sameness because the people of suburbia are predominantly white, middle-class, and under fifty years of age. Big city life is varied, exciting, and culturally stimulating. However, the nation's big cities are also overcrowded, crime-ridden, overcast with air pollution, short on public recreational facilities, and lacking in neighborhood spirit. The city dweller is often an anonymous figure unknown to the person living next door.

Although the majority of families live in homes, many

live in apartment buildings. These range in size from walk-ups containing from two to six apartments to high-rise elevator buildings that may have more than 100 apartments. Some high-rise apartments are very expensive and elegant, but many are built for moderate or even low-income families.

More than 7 million Americans live in *mobile homes* (once called *house trailers*). Mobile homes are living quarters built with wheels. They can be moved, but generally they are brought to a site that is intended to be more or less permanent. Then the wheels are removed, and the home is fastened to the ground. Because they cost much less than conventional homes, mobile homes are especially popular among young couples and elderly retired couples. Usually, the mobile home itself is paid for in installments, and the site is rented. Some experts predict that by 1983 about 20 million Americans will be living in mobile homes.

Of the nation's 71 million dwelling units, 64 percent are occupied by their owners. Though most homes are owned by their residents, some are rented. Apartments are usually rented, but in recent years increasing numbers of apartment buildings have become *cooperatives*, meaning that each resident owns his own apartment.

About 87 percent of American families are headed by a married couple. We like to think of the typical American household as being closer to a democracy than to a dictatorship. Ideally, Mother and Father have an equal voice in decision-making, and, on certain matters, the children, too, have a vote (perhaps at weekly family council meetings). That is the ideal, but obviously not all households are run this way. Many families still live by the old principle that Father's word is law. In many others, Father is rarely home when the children are awake, and, as far as the children are concerned, Mother is the dominant personality and major decision-maker.

Then, there are about 3 million households (with about 8 million children) in which one parent is absent as a result of separation, divorce, or desertion. Almost 90 percent of these households are headed by women whose children spend relatively little time with their fathers. In these families, Mother is boss.

In many other households, the children seem to be in charge. Some parents are reluctant and perhaps even afraid to say "no" to their children for fear of stifling their personalities or losing their love. As a result, the children and their possessions take over most of the house, and the youngsters make excessive demands upon their parents' time and money. In these families, the adults often suffer in silence, believing that they are doing "the right thing" for their children. The children suffer, too, lacking the security of strong, decisive parents who set appropriate limits and provide intelligent guidance.

For better or worse, Americans are devoted and permissive parents—so much so, in fact, that they are often accused of creating a child-centered culture. The ambitions of American parents are more often related to their children's lives than to their own. For this reason, parents often turn to the writings of experts—pediatricians, psychiatrists, and psychologists—for advice on child-rearing.

Because they believe that knowledge leads to a meaningful life, American parents try to give their youngsters many opportunities to develop skills and worthwhile interests. The typical middle-class child has a large assortment of educational toys and athletic equipment. He may also receive instruction in sports and music. To help him do well in school, he may be given his own room and desk, a set of encyclopedia, and, if necessary, private tutoring.

When school lets out for the summer, parents try to give their children other kinds of learning experiences through camping or travel. Family automobile trips to places of historical interest, national parks, and resort areas are commonplace. Summer day camps and residential camps are popular with American youngsters. They provide supervised group play, nature study, and instruction in crafts and athletics.

Parental roles have altered somewhat since the advent of the working mother. Today, about 10 million American mothers with children under eighteen years of age have jobs. In some families, the working mother is a necessity because the father is unable to find employment or cannot earn enough for all the family's basic needs. In other households, the mother may work to supplement the father's income so the family can enjoy a higher standard of living. Then, too, some women want to work even if the family does not need extra income. Once their children are attending school, many women find it boring to stay home alone all day. Being a homemaker is no longer a full-time job for women who have access to modern household appliances and prepared foods. Many working mothers employ a cleaning woman one or more days a week to help with housework and child care, but few have live-in servants.

When a working mother has no household help, her husband often takes a more active part in housekeeping and child-rearing. But even in families where the mother does not have an outside job, the father typically spends a significant amount of his leisure time with his children. He will often take a special interest in teaching his youngsters athletic skills. On weekends, especially, the family is likely to spend time together—attending church, visiting relatives, watching a ball game, going bike-riding, touring the zoo, or just playing "catch" in the backyard while the hamburgers are barbecuing. On weekends, Dad may try hard to be a pal to his children. However, during the week his children may see him very little. He may leave home early in the morning and come back when it's almost bedtime for the youngsters.

The various tensions, arguments, and hostilities which exist within the family are reflected in the well-known expression: "God gives us our relatives; thank God we can choose our friends." Conflicts between husband and wife and conflicts between different generations develop for many different reasons. One of the most common causes of quarrels is insufficient family income. Foreigners may think that Americans have more money than they know what to do with, but most Americans feel that they do not have enough. The median family income in the United States is about $11,000 a year. This is not a lot of money when one realizes the tremendous number of American needs. Products that most people did not even dream of thirty-five years ago (such as home airconditioners, TVs, and electric dishwashers) are now desired by nearly everyone. In most families, there is a shortage of money to supply all the things that family members consider essential for enjoyable, comfortable modern living.

In addition to the need for possessions, there are a great many costly services which most parents want to give their children, such as good medical and dental care, religious training, music lessons, and a college education. Parents may quarrel between themselves or with their children about priorities; and when there isn't enough to go around, the wife may secretly resent her husband for being an inadequate provider. More often, she decides to go to work. Teen-age children, too, often work part time after school, perhaps babysitting, selling, waiting on tables, mowing lawns, or delivering newspapers. Clearly, the need for many material things strongly influences the way American families live.

Concerning money or anything else, conflicts between husband and wife usually reflect a power struggle. Conflicts between parent and child often center around the same issue. As children enter adolescence, they begin to demand greater freedom to go where they please, do what they please, and make decisions without parental interference. Many American parents do not know how to deal with their teen-agers and seek advice from books, lectures, and parent-training courses. Parents want to maintain a friendly relationship with their teen-agers and also want to guide them so that their behavior will be whatever the parents consider proper and constructive. But in a society of rapidly changing social and moral values, parents and children often disagree about what is important and what is right. Arguments may concern such unimportant matters as styles of dress or hairdos. But quarrels may also concern school work, after-school jobs, decisions about how the teen-ager spends his money, career decisions, use of the family car, dating, and sexual behavior. Some families have serious problems with teen-agers who drop out of school, run away from home, or use illegal drugs. Because so much publicity is given to the problem teen-ager, one gets the impression that all teen-agers are troublemakers. Actually, relatively few adolescents do anything outrageously wrong, and nearly all grow up into "solid citizens" who fulfill most of their parents' expectations. In fact, recent studies show that the "generation gap" is narrowing. The vast majority of teen-agers share most of their parents' values and ideas. Many parents of teen-agers feel that they get along with their adolescents quite well.

The "generation gap" also causes problems between married children and their parents. The mother-in-law is the butt of many jokes. Seemingly, no one can get along with her because (according to the stereotype) she is an interfering busybody always criticizing what the younger generation is doing and sure that she knows a better way. Because of the stereotype, many mothers-in-law are afraid to make any suggestions at all to their married children. But many do interfere simply because they have little else to do. Women who have devoted their adult years exclusively to child-rearing may find it difficult to be left with an "empty nest." In addition, many middle-aged and elderly women are widows, since most American wives outlive their husbands by several years. The mother-in-law who cannot occupy herself with a job, volunteer work, hobbies, or social activities may become a too-frequent and sometimes unwelcome visitor in the homes of her children.

Middle age is a problem for some Americans, but for many others it is a pleasurable period of life, a time when they enjoy the fruits of their earlier labors—a comfortable income, a nice family, professional accomplishment. Most of the leadership in all areas of American life comes from middle-aged people.

For the elderly, however, life is often quite trying. In addition to the medical problems that inevitably come with old age, there are great economic and social problems. The difficulties of older Americans have been getting more attention in recent years as the elderly have increased in number. There are now 21 million Americans sixty-five years or older.

In many stable societies, older people are highly respected because of their experience and wisdom. But in a rapidly changing industrial society, the skills and knowledge of the elderly often become obsolete. The elderly American, commonly forced to retire from his job at age sixty-five, is left with too much leisure time and too little money. About 40 percent of the nation's elderly live in poverty or near-poverty. Many struggle along on the meager monthly income they get from the government by living in run-down hotels and eating mostly soup, potatoes, and bread. There are several government programs to supply free food and necessary services to the elderly. However, these programs do not reach anything close to the number of people who need help. As a result, there are probably millions of elderly Americans who live in isolation and misery.

The news media, in describing the plight of the elderly poor, sometimes create the false impression that Americans are heartless people who discard their aged parents and leave them to struggle alone in illness and poverty. Most old people are not dumped into nursing homes and mental institutions and forgotten. More than half of the elderly in the United States live in their own homes, with one of their children, or with friends. Many who live alone do so by choice. Some live in special buildings or small communities established for the elderly. These communities usually have many kinds of recreational facilities and a doctor or nurse on duty at all times.

Despite the euphemisms which refer to "senior citizens" enjoying their "golden years," one finds that in this society which worships youth, the elderly are sometimes ignored or even avoided. American society provides a monthly income and free medical care to the aged, but it often deprives them of important psychological forms of support—a feeling of being respected, wanted, and needed.

Many older people find more satisfactory social relationships among other "senior citizens" than among members of their own family. However, within the family, one often sees strong bonds between grandparents and grandchildren. American family life has been much enriched by medical advances which have prolonged life. An American boy born in 1970 can be expected to live to age sixty-seven, a girl to age seventy-five. Most of today's children have living grandparents and many have living great-grandparents.

Another problem facing the nuclear family (mother, father, and dependent children) is the fact that it is expected to do too much. Years ago, families settled down in a particular residence and stayed there for many years. Often, other relatives (grandparents, aunts, uncles, cousins) lived nearby and were part of the daily scene. Close bonds with neighbors developed, providing lifelong friendships. Today, Americans are extremely mobile. Every year about 40 million Americans change residences. That statistic suggests that everyone moves every five or six years! Young people from farms and small towns come to the big cities for excitement and job opportunities. Couples with young children move from cities to suburbs to provide a safer, more spacious environment for their children and a better school system. Southern blacks and Appalachian whites move to northern industrial areas like Chicago and Detroit in search of full-time employment and higher wages. All this shifting around puts a great burden upon family members sharing one household. They must supply the psychological support that was once provided by a much larger group, and many families cannot do it.

In some ways, the family as an institution fails its members. However, there are certainly a great many happy families; and, although people complain about and quarrel with members of their family, when trouble arises, close relatives are usually the first to step in and help. Americans frequently say, "Blood is thicker than water."

Although the family remains the basic social unit, an extremely small percentage of Americans have chosen communal living instead. There are now about 3,000 communes in the United States, involving about 100,000 members. The news media have widely publicized this lifestyle, and some experts have predicted that it is the wave of the future. However, other experts point out that communal movements have existed in the past, and yet the family has always survived.

By most definitions, a commune is a socialistic community in which people who are not all related by either blood or marriage share living quarters. One broad definition is "a group of persons associated together for the purpose of establishing an integrated way of life." This may include vocational, cultural, educational, and spiritual activities.

There are many different types of communes involving many different kinds of members. There are both rural and urban communes, some with fewer than a dozen members, some with well over a hundred. There are communes for the young, the elderly, and for mixed age groups. However, the vast majority of commune members are between the ages of eighteen and forty. Communes may be composed of single people, groups of families, or mixtures of both. Many communes have fallen apart within a year after their establishment; others have been in existence for several years. Some are able to support themselves comfortably by selling products they make or grow. Some send their members to work outside the commune. Some struggle to "live off the land," to survive on whatever food they can grow and raise themselves.

Some could not survive without financial assistance from relatives. Members of a commune may share one major interest, for example, crafts, agriculture, or a particular spiritual or religious faith. Some communes practice homosexuality and some group marriage.

Certain attitudes are widespread among commune members. First, there is the belief that great changes are needed in our social and institutional structures to stop the dehumanization of man. Members feel that communes improve society by bringing people close together through love and understanding. Second, commune members are very much concerned about ecology and have a deep reverence for nature. Third, there is in communal living a rejection of materialism, a distaste for the consumption-oriented American society. Fourth, there is the belief that life should be enjoyable and work should be a pleasurable form of self-expression. These same attitudes and interests are also widespread among young Americans following more traditional living patterns.

The communal movement, viewed as a possible substitute for family life, has been much talked about, both favorably and unfavorably. Whatever its future may be, communal living is presently outside the mainstream of American life. On the other hand, the American family helps to prepare the coming generation to function successfully in a complex, competitive, democratic society. As in all other nations, in the United States family life is the basis of individual security and cultural continuity.

EXERCISES

Comprehension. Choose the correct answer.

1. American families tend to have
   (a) one child.
   (b) two to three children.
   (c) five or more children.

2. Most Americans live
   (a) on farms.
   (b) in communes.
   (c) in or near big cities.

3. High-rise apartment buildings always have
   (a) elevators.
   (b) cooperatives.
   (c) low-income tenants.

4. Most American families are headed by
   (a) a dictator.
   (b) a married couple.
   (c) communes.

5. The term *senior citizens* refers to
   (a) teen-agers.
   (b) parents.
   (c) persons over 65.

6. American family ties are weakened by
   (a) mobility.
   (b) marriage.
   (c) middle age.

7. American workers are commonly forced to retire from their jobs at age
   (a) fifty.
   (b) sixty-five.
   (c) seventy-five.

8. The *generation gap* refers to
   (a) differences between children and parents.
   (b) the years between childhood and adulthood.
   (c) the lack of money caused by raising children.

9. At birth, the life expectancy of the American woman is about
   (a) fifty-two.
   (b) sixty-four.
   (c) seventy-five.

10. Communal living is
    (a) rapidly replacing the family.

(b) materialistic.
(c) an attempt at improving society.

Vocabulary and Usage. Give the meaning of each of the following words. Use each in a sentence.

urban	residential
rural	access
suburb	priority
cooperative	resent
high-rise	ecology

Conversation and Discussion. What attitudes about child-rearing are widespread in the United States? Do these differ from child-rearing practices of other countries?

IV
The American Economy

CAPITALISM—ITS WEAKNESSES AND STRENGTHS

The United States is a capitalistic country. To Americans, capitalism is not a political philosophy; it is an economic system. In a capitalistic economy, businesses are owned and operated by private enterprise. Competition, supply, and demand determine prices and wages. In general, the role of government is not to operate or regulate businesses but to function as a neutral force protecting each element of the economy—big business, small business, workers, and consumers—from abuse.

In the United States, privately owned companies, not the federal government, provide for basic needs such as fuel, banking services, and facilities for transportation and communication (though in many cities, transportation facilities are owned and operated by city governments). However, these major industries are closely regulated by the government to assure the public safe, dependable, and honest service. Regarding other industries, governmental controls are more limited; they exist primarily to safeguard public health, encourage competition, and protect children who work.

In a capitalistic economy, prices fluctuate freely in response to supply and demand. In other words, when there are more apples available than people want to buy, the price of apples goes down; when there is a shortage, the price goes up. In the United States, the government does exercise some control over prices through taxation, the federal banking system, subsidies and price supports (especially to farmers), and by increases or decreases in its own expenditures. Despite these controls, within the past thirty-five years both prices and wages have risen steadily.

Under ideal conditions, a free competitive economy is beneficial to everyone. The worker can choose the career he wants to follow; he can change jobs in pursuit of higher wages, better working conditions, or professional advancement; and he can unite with other workers to demand better treatment from his employer. The manufacturer or merchant profits when his business is successful.

However, in order to compete in an open market, he must operate efficiently, economically, and creatively. Because of competition among businesses, the customer receives high-quality merchandise at the lowest possible prices.

Of course, American capitalism is not ideal. Weaknesses in the system sometimes create temporary national crises and long-term injustices. Two common problems which plague the American economy are difficulties in maintaining competition and threats to public welfare due to strikes of dissatisfied workers.

In some industries, small businesses are unable to compete with giant corporations that provide goods faster, cheaper, and in greater variety. Sometimes a large company monopolizes a particular service or product. When there is inadequate competition in an industry, the public suffers, since it is competition that forces companies to keep quality high and prices low.

When a strike occurs in a vital industry, it can disrupt the entire economy. An example is the frequent threat of a railroad strike which would force the shutdown of manufacturing companies that depend upon rail service for delivery of raw materials. Employees of these factories would be laid off and forced to curtail their spending. This, in turn, would adversely affect the incomes of merchants who usually sell to these unemployed workers. When workers go on strike, the public may be seriously inconvenienced also. Strikes can shut down transportation or cut off food or fuel supplies to large areas.

Still, despite all the problems of American business, this nation has achieved an economy of unequaled abundance. At one time, capitalism was considered an evil system which brought great wealth to the few by exploiting the majority. But contemporary American capitalism is profitable for workers as well as owners. Few Americans holding full-time, year-round jobs are poor. Instead, poor Americans are those who, either because of old age, illness, disability, or lack of skills, cannot work full time. To most of the population, capitalism has brought prosperity.

CORPORATIONS AND THE STOCK MARKET

In the United States, the trend is toward large-scale production that can efficiently and economically service the needs of many customers. For this purpose, vast amounts of money are needed to acquire land, build factories, buy equipment and raw materials, and hire labor. Where does all this money come from? It does not come from the government, since one of the basic characteristics of capitalism is private ownership of business. Very few major enterprises are owned and operated by the federal government. Telephone service, radio and TV stations, railroads, airlines—all of these huge industries are made up of competing companies that sell their stock to the American public. These stockholders own and control most of the nation's business.

Much of American business is handled by corporations. A corporation is an artificial entity created by law. It can buy and sell property, lend or borrow money, employ people, enter into contracts, and generally perform the same business dealings that an individual can. The corporation raises money by selling its stock. Purchasers of this stock become owners of the corporation in proportion to the amount of stock they buy. For example, if a corporation wished to raise $1,000, it could sell 100 shares of stock at $10 each. For every ten shares of stock purchased, the buyer would acquire ownership of one-tenth of the corporation. As one of the owners, he would have a right to share in the corporation's profits and help choose its management.

Large corporations must raise huge amounts of capital. To do so, they sell their stock on a massive scale to anyone who wants to buy it. American Telephone and Telegraph, for example, has about 550 million shares outstanding, which are owned by more than three million stockholders.

If a person has extra money to invest, he can purchase a share in almost any industry he chooses by buying stock at one of the stock exchanges. The stock of about 3,000 corporations is sold on the major exchanges. The oldest and largest of these is the New York Stock Exchange. This exchange, along with several of the nation's largest banks, is located in Manhattan on Wall Street. Thus, the term *Wall Street* has become a synonym for American financial interests.

Stock prices often reflect the health of the economy. When business conditions are good, stock prices tend to rise, creating what is called a *bull market*. When conditions are poor or threatening, prices drop, creating a *bear market*. News items often have a marked temporary effect upon the market. For example, stock prices fell rapidly the Friday that President Kennedy was assassinated. By the time the market reopened the following week, public confidence had been restored and prices rose to new highs.

Because of the inflationary nature of the American economy, every year more and more Americans invest in stocks. As prices of food, clothing, and everything else rise, the prices of stocks also tend to rise. In terms of 1944 purchasing power, today's dollar is worth only about 50 cents. However, in that same period, the stock prices comprising one of the popular indexes quintupled!

In 1952, only about 6.5 million Americans were shareholders. Twenty years later, the figure was 32.5 million (almost one out of every six). At least another 76 million have invested in stocks indirectly through their participation in pension plans and life insurance policies. Not only the wealthy invest in stocks. Some 58 percent of all shareholders report annual family incomes of less than $15,000. Although many people who buy and sell stocks on a daily basis lose money, most long-term investors have profited. The stock market enables millions of middle-class Americans to share in the prosperity of American business and spreads the nation's wealth among an ever-increasing percentage of the population.

Stocks are one popular type of investment; another is called *bonds*. The person who buys stocks is actually purchasing a portion of a particular company. The person who invests in bonds is merely making a loan. The bond itself is the borrower's written promise to repay the loan on a certain date and also to pay a certain rate of interest on the borrowed money. The individual who buys bonds does not share in the company's profits, but neither does he run the risk of losing money if the stock goes down in value. Corporations may issue bonds to obtain money for expansion. State and local governments issue bonds to raise funds for community improvements such as highways, bridges, schools, and hospitals. Even the United States government borrows money from individuals. U. S. savings bonds are available in various denominations and are often purchased as gifts. A government E bond bought today for $18.75 will be worth $25.00 in about seven years.

THE DOMINANCE OF BIG BUSINESS

Calvin Coolidge, President of the United States from

1923 to 1929, once said, "The business of America is business." This famous statement, expressing the importance of the marketplace to the total American way of life, is as true today as it was several decades ago. In the United States today, there are some 12 million business establishments, ranging from one-man newsstands to gigantic corporations employing tens of thousands. Experts estimate that about one-fourth of all urban workers have, at some time, been in business for themselves. Small businesses—farms, clothing stores, bakery and butcher shops, cleaning establishments, gas stations, restaurants—are a significant part of American capitalism. Nevertheless, the nation's economy is dominated by big business. Approximately 500,000 corporations handle about 75 percent of the nation's business. Only 500 companies account for about one-third of all activity in the industrial field. Big business is quite aware of its own national importance, as indicated by the well-known remark, "What is good for General Motors is good for the United States, and vice versa."

To what extent is the power of big business a corrupting power that poses a threat to the national welfare? At one time, the common concern was that workers and small businessmen were being exploited and sometimes destroyed by ruthless corporate giants. Now, labor unions protect employees and, to some extent, laws protect both workers and small businessmen. But who protects the consumer? Big business, concerned more about profits than public welfare, can harm people in many ways. In recent years, there have been widespread protests about corporate crimes, including the production of deceitful ads, unsafe products, and dangerous levels of pollution.

Also, the ability of big business to influence governmental decisions is an obvious evil. Political candidates and parties seek the financial support of wealthy business leaders, who often buy political favors by making substantial contributions to the candidates' campaigns. Corporate financial power is capable of influencing governmental decisions in local, national, and even international affairs.

THE CONSUMER WITHOUT CASH

In this country, a huge assortment of merchandise is available at prices the average worker can afford. In addition, products and services are continually becoming easier to buy, and the quality, in general, is improving. Consequently, more and more consumers are purchasing more and more products. Even expensive items such as television sets, refrigerators, airconditioners, and automobiles are within the purchasing power of most workers. Those who can't pay for them immediately can buy them on credit. A $3,000 automobile can be purchased with very little cash and paid for over a three-year period at about $85 a month. Other expensive items—homes, furniture, appliances—are frequently paid for in monthly installments.

In addition to installment buying, many people use credit cards to "buy now and pay later." To make a purchase on credit, the customer gives his credit card to the salesman, who fills out a charge sales slip and returns the card to the purchaser. At the end of each month, the customer receives a bill showing the charges he has made during that period. The customer must pay the balance within three or four weeks. If he is late in making his payment, he is usually charged interest on the amount owed. Most credit card issuers permit the user to pay a small portion of the total due instead of paying the entire balance; but if he does this, he is charged interest on the balance.

Two types of credit cards are in common use. One type is issued by a particular store and can be used only at the issuer's place of business. The customer pays the bill directly to the store he purchased from. The other type is issued by a bank or other credit institution and may be used at any establishment that agrees to honor it. The bank pays the store for the merchandise (less a discount) when the merchant presents the sales slip to the bank. If the customer doesn't pay his bill, the bank rather than the merchant suffers the loss.

Credit privileges have been abused by many people. As a result, since 1960 the annual number of wage-earner bankruptcies has more than tripled. But for those who do not burden themselves with more monthly bills than they can handle, credit buying is a boon. It has enabled Americans to enjoy comforts they could not otherwise afford and has helped to make the American standard of living the highest in the world.

Another common method of paying for merchandise or services is by check. Most American families maintain checking accounts so that they do not have to carry large amounts of cash with them. A check is simply a written order to a bank to transfer money belonging to the check writer to someone else. The check indicates how much is to be paid and to whom. If the check is lost or stolen, it can easily be replaced. A check can be safely sent by mail and also provides proof of payment in case of a dispute. Because of the widespread use of checking accounts and credit cards, the United States has become known as a cashless society.

* * *

American capitalism, with all its problems, has proved to be the most productive economic system in human history. In addition, the freedom of choice it provides appeals strongly to the independent American disposition. No central authority dictates what or how much should be produced, although in a few industries the federal government offers incentives to encourage production of needed goods. With few exceptions, no external power tells a businessman how much to charge for his goods or services. For the most part, everyone is free to decide how he will earn and spend his income. Although the American government does place some controls upon the nation's economy, the United States gives its citizens greater economic freedom than do most other countries.

The American economic system is based upon the beliefs that every individual knows what is best for himself and that everyone must accept responsibility for his own decisions. The risk exists, but so does the opportunity for advancement. Most Americans gladly accept both.

EXERCISES

Comprehension. Choose the correct answer.

1. In the United States, capitalism is
   (a) an economic system.
   (b) a governmental system.
   (c) a means of production.

2. In a capitalistic economy, government
   (a) plays a large role.
   (b) owns businesses.
   (c) plays a small role.

3. In the United States, prices are regulated by
   (a) the government.
   (b) Wall Street.
   (c) supply and demand.

4. Installment buying is a form of
   (a) credit.
   (b) cash.
   (c) check.

5. Much American business is handled by
   (a) the government.
   (b) corporations.
   (c) socialism.

6. Corporations raise capital by selling
   (a) stock.
   (b) credit.
   (c) government.

7. Bonds are issued
   (a) only by the federal government.
   (b) only by corporations.
   (c) by both businesses and governments.

8. When a person buys stock in a corporation, he becomes
   (a) a consumer.
   (b) a worker.
   (c) an owner.

9. The New York Stock Exchange is located on
   (a) Broadway.
   (b) Wall Street.
   (c) Easy Street.

10. Under conditions of inflation, prices
   (a) rise.
   (b) fall.
   (c) remain the same.

Vocabulary and Usage. Give the meaning of each of the following words. Use each word in a sentence.

competition	capitalism	bankruptcy
control	economy	subsidy
stock	inflation	expenditure
credit	debt	monopolize
interest	corporation	entity

Conversation and Discussion. What are stocks? Why does a corporation sell them? Why do people buy them?

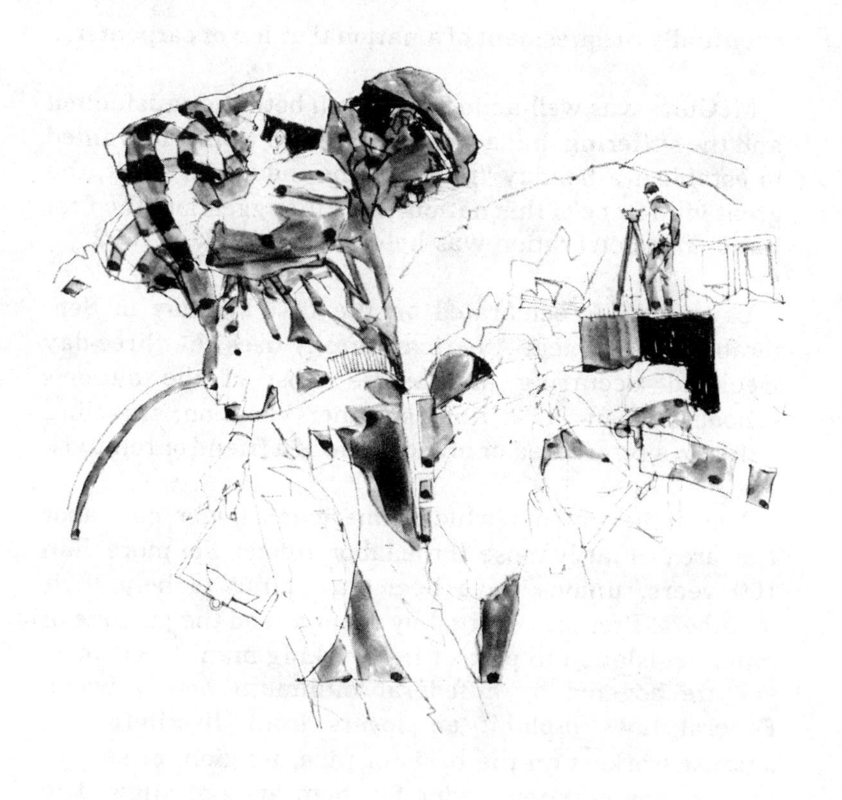

V
Labor Day and the American Worker

The story of Labor Day began in the nineteenth century with the dream of a carpenter named Peter J. McGuire. McGuire was born in 1852, long before the United States had laws prohibiting child labor. He was the tenth child in a poor family. To help support his brothers and sisters, he went to work in a furniture factory when he was only eleven years old. He grew up to become a carpenter and eventually the president of a national union of carpenters.

McGuire was well-acquainted with both the satisfaction and the suffering that accompanies hard work. He wanted to establish a holiday "to honor the industrial spirit, the great vital force of this nation." At his suggestion, the first Labor Day celebration was held in New York in 1892.

Labor Day is celebrated on the first Monday in September. The typical American family uses the three-day weekend—occurring just before most of the nation's schools reopen—as a final summer vacation, traveling either to a resort area or to the home of a friend or relative.

The achievements which Americans honor on Labor Day are primarily those of the labor unions. For more than 100 years, unions have been struggling to help their members. Pressure exerted by them forced the passage of much legislation to protect the working man. Most workers are covered by a federal minimum hourly wage. Federal laws prohibit employers from discriminating against workers on the basis of race, religion, or sex. In most states children under fourteen are not allowed to hold jobs, though there are a few exceptions to this restriction which enable youngsters to deliver newspapers or work as entertainers.

American unions have fought continuously for higher wages, a shorter work week, extra pay for overtime work, paid vacations, sick leave, health insurance, pension plans, and safe, sanitary working conditions. Now, unions are supporting the concept of the guaranteed annual income. Thanks to the perseverance of organized labor, the American worker is one of the best paid and best cared for in the world. About 20 million persons—more than one-fourth of the non-agricultural workers in the United States—belong to labor unions. There are unions for miners, musicians, teachers, janitors, nurses, plumbers, and dozens of other occupational groups and industries.

In attempting to achieve its goals, a union may employ the most powerful weapon that it possesses: the strike. A strike occurs when union members decide not to return to work until their employer gives in to some or all of their demands. Workers on strike *picket* their employer by walking back and forth in front of his place of business, carrying signs stating their complaints. The custom of picketing has also been adopted by other protest groups to make known their disapproval of particular policies of government or industry.

There are now almost 200 national unions in the United States. As unions grew in size and number, federal legislation was needed to protect business and the national economy from the dominance of organized labor. In 1947, the Taft-Hartley Labor Act was passed to help maintain a balance of power between labor and management.

Today, the American employee has good reason to celebrate Labor Day. Working a comparatively short work week, he can still afford to buy a vast number of items to make his life comfortable and pleasurable. The average work week (thirty-seven hours) is shorter for Americans than for Europeans. The forty-hour week (eight hours per day, five days a week) is considered standard here, but, from one industry to another, regular full-time employment ranges from thirty-five to forty-two hours per week. Most employees are paid at a higher hourly rate when they work overtime.

Compared to his grandfather and great-grandfather, the contemporary American worker is quite fortunate. In 1900, the average work week was sixty hours; in 1850, it was nearly seventy hours! And, of course, the purchasing power of today's worker far exceeds his ancestors'.

Even within the last two decades, purchasing power has increased, especially for major household appliances. In 1955, it took one hundred forty-six hours of high average earnings to buy a new washing machine, compared to sixty-seven hours in 1973. The cost in labor of electric ranges and refrigerators showed a similar decline.

Between 1959 and 1973, median family income leaped from about $5,000 to more than $11,000 a year. This big jump was due, in part, to the influx of married women into the labor market. However, individual income has also been rising within the last few decades. By 1971, a production worker in manufacturing was earning an average of $3.57 per hour including overtime. He worked about four minutes to buy a loaf of bread, ten minutes to buy a half gallon of milk, twenty-three hours to buy a new suit, and about eight weeks to buy a good used car.

Compared to workers in other nations, the typical American worker is rich. The average American earns almost twice as much in real wages as workers in any other nation. The average American works twelve minutes to earn enough money to buy a dozen eggs. To make the same purchase, the average Englishman works about sixty minutes, the Frenchman one hundred and eight minutes. In Moscow, the average man works eleven hours to buy a cotton shirt; the New Yorker works less than two hours. American purchasing power is about five or six times as great as the world's average, about twice that of Western Europe, and about ten times that of Asia. Most American families live comfortably and have plenty of food and clothing. About 83 percent of families own at least one automobile. Nearly all households are equipped with indoor plumbing, electricity, central heating, a telephone, a TV set, and major kitchen appliances such as a stove and refrigerator.

American workers are now enjoying more leisure time and larger periods of leisure time than ever before. About 95 percent of industrial workers receive paid vacations. Nearly 25 percent of them get three weeks off with pay. In 1971, the dates of four national holidays were changed so that they would always be celebrated on Mondays. These changes have given most employees at least five three-day weekends each year, including the Labor Day weekend. The idea of the long weekend is so appealing that hundreds of industrial plants are trying it on a regular basis. By lengthening the working day to ten or twelve hours, the work week can be shortened to four or even three days.

The American worker is protected in many ways from sudden stoppage of income. If a worker is "laid off" through no fault of his own, he may be eligible for *unemployment compensation*—temporary payments from the government—until he finds another job. Another way in which a worker can protect his paycheck is by purchasing insurance that guarantees his family a regular income if the "breadwinner" dies or cannot continue working because of injury or illness. About 80 percent of American families invest in some type of life insurance policy, and many also have disability insurance.

But the most widespread type of financial protection comes in the form of a federal program called *social security.* Nine out of ten working people in the United States are building protection for themselves and their families through social security. During their working years, employees, their employers, and self-employed people contribute to the social security fund. Then, when earnings stop or are reduced because of retirement, disability, or death, the worker or his family receives monthly cash payments to replace part of the lost income.

Nearly all employees and self-employed persons are

required to participate in the social security program. The employed person's contribution is deducted from his wages each payday. The self-employed person pays his contribution quarterly. The employee earning less than $12,000 a year pays almost six percent of his salary to social security, and his employer pays an equal amount. The self-employed person in the same income bracket pays nearly eight percent of his annual earnings. A record of each worker's lifetime earnings is maintained by the government under his social security number.

A worker must contribute to the fund a specified length of time in order to be eligible for social security benefits. The amount of money received depends upon the individual's average earnings during his working years. Payments range from less than $100 a month for an individual to more than $600 a month for a family. Social security benefits have been increased periodically as the nation's standard of living has climbed. Although benefits are far from lavish, they do provide the retired or disabled worker with funds for essential needs.

Male workers who retire usually begin receiving monthly social security checks at age sixty-five. Women become eligible at sixty-two. Retired workers may choose to begin receiving payments a few years earlier, but then the amount received each month is smaller. A person does not have to stop working completely to collect his full social security check. However, if his earnings exceed a certain amount, his social security benefits may be reduced.

Since 1965, the social security system has also included health insurance commonly called *Medicare*. Under this program, people sixty-five or older who are covered by social security are also covered by free hospitalization insurance. These people can also obtain additional insurance to cover outpatient medical expenses. This additional insurance is financed by premiums paid equally by the federal government and people who enroll. Many people sixty-five or older are eligible for Medicare, even though they might not have enough work credit to receive social security cash benefits.

The social security system also provides special payments to people over age seventy-two who are not eligible for regular benefits. Another federal program, administered although not funded by the Social Security Administration, guarantees a minimum monthly income to people who are sixty-five or older, blind, or disabled.

In addition to social security protection, some 30 to 35 million American workers (at least one-third of the nation's work force) are in jobs covered by private retirement plans. About five million retired workers are now receiving pensions from their former employers.

For most Americans, Labor Day is an occasion to pause and count their blessings. Unfortunately, the total picture of the American economy contains some dark spots. The United States is the most prosperous nation in the world, but in the midst of prosperity for the majority, about 24 million Americans are living below what the federal government considers the poverty level (presently about $4,300 a year for a nonfarm family of four). The percentage of poverty-level American families has declined from about 60 percent in 1914 to about 13 percent today. Nonetheless, there is deep national concern about the deprivation of the poor.

In the North and West, poverty tends to be concentrated in the cities, while in the South most poverty is rural. Most poor Americans fall into one or more of the following categories: the elderly retired; the disabled; unskilled workers and their families; the uneducated; the unemployed; and nonwhites. Although federal funds provide for the elderly and the disabled, these benefits are small. The unemployed person living solely on a federal pension must budget himself very strictly. Although blacks comprise only 11 percent of the national population, they constitute 32 percent of the poor. In 1970, 20 percent of nonwhite families had incomes under $3,000; only 7.5 percent of white families had incomes that low.

Since a large percentage of the poor are those who can't find jobs, there has been much concern about the nation's high unemployment rate. This figure indicates the percentage of people between the ages of sixteen and sixty-five who seek employment and cannot find it. The unemployment rate generally fluctuates between three and five percent. However, in recent years it has often been close to five percent and has sometimes gone higher. There are usually three to five million unemployed, job-hunting Americans. Automation has stolen jobs from thousands of workers as factories continue to replace more and more men with machines. Workers who are unskilled or who possess obsolete skills must be trained for new types of work. Jobs are somewhat harder to find for the person who is uneducated, unskilled, nonwhite, female, or a teenager. However, even men in skilled or professional job categories have difficulties finding suitable jobs if they live in areas where workers with their kind of training are plentiful; yet in many of the skilled and semi-skilled trades, there is a shortage of qualified job applicants. Both problems could be relieved by training some of the unemployed to fill these vacant positions. Better transportation for urban workers who want suburban jobs would help to ease the unemployment situation, too.

In recent years, at least the numbers of poor have declined. In 1959, more than 39 million Americans were living in poverty. In 1964, the figure was 36 million. In the early 1970s, it was about 24 million (about one out of every nine Americans).

For those who remain poor, the government offers many forms of assistance. About 14 million Americans depend upon public welfare programs for their livelihood. These include children whose parents cannot adequately support them and parents who cannot hold jobs because of inadequate skills or because they are needed at home to care for small children. Programs operated by local welfare agencies include aid to families with dependent children (commonly referred to as ADC or AFDC), old-age assistance, aid to the blind, and aid to the permanently and totally disabled. Public assistance, financed jointly by the federal government and state and local governments, provides three main kinds of help: money, medical care (through a program called *Medicaid*), and social services to help people solve problems concerning family life, housing, job training, and education.

Labor Day is no occasion for rejoicing among poor and unemployed Americans. Nor do most working women view their job situation as ideal. When in competition with equally qualified men, women are less likely to be hired, more likely to be fired if business slows down, and less likely to be promoted to a position of greater responsibility, authority, and income. Also, many women are paid less than men for doing the same jobs. The Women's Liberation movement has fought for legal protection that would help women receive a fair deal from employers. The Civil Rights Act of 1964 provides many working women with increased protection. However, it does not cover all industries or all types of jobs. Under consideration now is a Constitutional amendment called the Equal Rights Amendment (ERA) which would give the federal government the authority to prohibit the kind of job discrimination that has victimized women. This amendment has already been approved by Congress and some of the states. If thirty-eight of the fifty states approve the measure, it will become the 27th Amendment to the federal Constitution.

To increase and equalize opportunities for American workers, many changes are needed, and many concerned people are struggling to bring these changes about. We look forward to the time when Labor Day may truly be a day of rejoicing for all American workers.

EXERCISES

Comprehension. Choose the correct answer.

1. Peter McGuire was a
   (a) teacher.
   (b) carpenter.
   (c) businessman.

2. Labor Day celebrates the achievement of
   (a) carpenters.
   (b) businessmen.
   (c) labor unions.

3. A union's most powerful weapon is the
   (a) strike.
   (b) picket.
   (c) lockout.

4. Union activities are controlled by the
   (a) Civil Rights Act of 1964.
   (b) Taft-Hartley Labor Act.
   (c) Bill of Rights.

5. The median family income in the U.S.A. is about
   (a) $8,000.
   (b) $11,000.
   (c) $5,000.

6. The average work week in the U.S.A. is
   (a) 48 hours.
   (b) 30 hours.
   (c) 37 hours.

7. Social security provides
   (a) pensions.
   (b) vacations.
   (c) employment.

8. Social security benefits are paid by
   (a) the federal government.
   (b) local welfare agencies.
   (c) unions.

9. A large part of the nation's poor people are
   (a) suburbanites.
   (b) nonwhite.
   (c) carpenters.

10. Many jobs have been taken over by
    (a) automation.
    (b) senior citizens.
    (c) the government.

Vocabulary and Usage. Give the meaning of each of the following words. Use each in a sentence.

labor	union
legislation	discrimination
picket	disability
automation	strike
benefit	unemployed

Conversation and Discussion. Discuss how labor unions have contributed to the welfare of the American worker.

VI
Columbus Day

Throughout most of the United States, Columbus Day is celebrated on the second Monday in October. The holiday honors Christopher Columbus, who is commonly called the discoverer of America. All of North and South America and some cities in Spain and Italy pay tribute to this brave explorer, although we know now that he was not the first European to land in the New World. Historians are convinced that Leif Ericson, an adventurous

Viking seaman, touched the coast of North America in 1000 A.D.—almost 500 years before Columbus' first voyage. But Leif Ericson's expedition did not have the same profound impact on world history; it was not followed by mass migrations and the development of the Americas, whereas Columbus' voyages opened the Western Hemisphere to first dozens, then millions of European settlers.

Christopher Columbus was born in 1451. He grew up in Genoa, an important Italian seaport. As a boy, he helped his father, a wool-weaver, by working at the loom. But while he weaved, he dreamed of a life at sea.

When he was about nineteen, Columbus began making sea voyages. In 1477, his travels brought him to Lisbon, Portugal, where his brother owned a map-making shop. Columbus settled down in Lisbon. He joined his brother's business and married a Portuguese girl. To please his wife, Columbus gave up his career as a sailor and became a map-maker. But when his wife died shortly after their son was born, Columbus began to think of the sea again.

During the fifteenth century, the Portuguese were looking for a sea route to the Indies. (At that time, the name *Indies* referred to India, China, the East Indies, and Japan.) They wanted to bring gold, jewels, spices, perfumes, and silks from the Orient back to Europe. When brought by land, these riches had to be loaded on camels to be carried across deserts. Caravans were often attacked and valuable goods were stolen. It would be easier, faster, and safer to import such luxuries by sea.

The Portuguese had tried to reach the Orient by sailing around Africa. Columbus thought he had a better route. He insisted that a ship could reach the East by sailing west. Columbus made only one important mistake: he underestimated the size of the earth. He never guessed that the huge continents of North and South America lay between Europe and Asia.

Columbus was *not* trying to prove that the world was round. The educated people of his time already knew that the earth was not flat. Columbus was simply looking for a short sea route to the East. He promised wealth and new territory to the king who would provide funds for his expedition. He also wanted fame and wealth for himself if his expedition succeeded.

The King of Portugal refused to pay for Columbus' explorations because the court's nautical experts advised against it. As a result, in 1485 Columbus and his young son, Diego, went to Spain to ask King Ferdinand and Queen Isabella for ships and sailors. The queen was sympathetic. She put Columbus on the royal payroll but could not equip him for the voyage while the Spanish were fighting the Moors. Columbus waited. His red hair turned gray. He developed arthritis. His savings dwindled, and his coat and shoes were so full of holes that he had to stay indoors when it rained.

In 1492, when the Spanish conquered Granada, Isabella was able to give more thought to Columbus' idea. Ferdinand did not want to spend the money because the recent wars had been very expensive. Isabella then offered to pawn her jewels in order to finance the trip. But this sacrifice was not necessary. The treasurer of Spain supplied most of the funds from the national treasury and from his own savings. The total investment, for which Columbus had waited seven years, was the equivalent of just $14,000!

For his first voyage, Columbus had three ships: the *Pinta*, the *Niña*, and the *Santa Maria*. The *Santa Maria*, which was the largest, was ninety feet long and carried a crew of forty. The entire crew of the fleet was about eighty-seven. The ships had good compasses but no instruments to measure distance. Fortunately, Columbus knew enough about celestial navigation to measure latitude by the North Star.

The fleet sailed from the Canary Islands on September 6, 1492. The crew lost sight of land on September 9. Then the ships sailed due west for three weeks, the longest anyone had ever sailed in one direction without seeing land. The sailors were frightened. They knew that the world was round, and they were not afraid of sailing too far and falling off the edge. But they were afraid that the winds from the east would keep them from reaching their destination and that all would die at sea. The crew begged Columbus to turn back; there were even whispers of mutiny.

On October 10, everyone agreed to sail on for three more days and then turn around if no land was seen. Columbus was optimistic. He had noticed some birds flying overhead and some seaweed floating on the water's surface. He felt certain that land must be nearby.

Before dawn on October 12, just thirty-six days after leaving the Canary Islands, the sailors were overjoyed to see white sand gleaming in the moonlight. Columbus' fleet was approaching an island in the Bahamas, an island which Columbus named San Salvador.

When the ships landed, the sailors were greeted by strange-looking people who wore no clothes. Because Columbus thought he had landed on an island of the Indies near Japan or China, he called these natives *Indians.* To this day, we refer to the islands which Columbus discovered and explored as the *West Indies.*

The three ships spent only a few days at San Salvador. Then they sailed on to Cuba and Haiti, where the *Santa Maria* was wrecked. On January 16, 1493, the *Pinta* and the *Niña* set sail for Spain. The voyage home was extremely rough, but Columbus was a brilliant navigator. On March 15, his ships arrived safely in Palos, Spain.

Columbus was a great national hero when he returned from this first expedition. But his popularity did not last. He made three more trips to explore the West Indies and South America. Some Spanish settlers remained in the new land to form a colony called Hispaniola (where Haiti and the Dominican Republic are now situated). These settlers had expected to find huge supplies of gold and other riches. Instead, they found primitive living conditions, strange foods, hard work, and constant danger. They blamed Columbus for their disappointment. Many went back to Spain and complained about him. Others stayed and rebelled against his leadership. The King and Queen sent a representative to settle the trouble in Hispaniola. The representative put Columbus and his brother in chains and sent them back to Spain for trial. When they arrived in Spain, the King and Queen freed them, but Columbus was replaced as governor of Hispaniola.

In a final attempt to regain his good name and wealth, Columbus began his fourth and last voyage. He left Spain in the spring of 1502 and returned in the winter of 1504. Before he could appear in court, Queen Isabella died. In great pain from arthritis, Columbus went to King Ferdinand to request the money and titles which he had been promised. The king would not grant his request.

During his last years, Columbus was a forgotten man with few friends and very little money. He was in much pain and scarcely able to move because of his arthritis. He died in 1506 at the age of fifty-four.

Columbus never realized that he had not reached the Orient but had instead discovered the New World. Not until 1521, when Magellan sailed around the entire globe, did Europeans learn that the territory which Columbus had explored was not in the Orient.

Although he was unappreciated during his lifetime, Columbus today is an international hero. American children love to retell and dramatize the exciting tale of his famous voyage in 1492. Columbus is admired for his courage, self-confidence, and perseverance. In school, many American children memorize a famous poem about Columbus. The closing lines explain what he symbolizes to the hemisphere he discovered:

> "He gained a world: he gave that world
> Its grandest lesson: 'On! Sail on!' "

EXERCISES

Comprehension. Choose the correct answer.

1. Christopher Columbus grew up in
   (a) Spain.
   (b) Portugal.
   (c) Italy.

2. On his first voyage, Columbus wanted to reach
   (a) the Orient.
   (b) the New World.
   (c) the West Indies.

3. During the fifteenth century, the name *Indies* referred to
   (a) the Middle East.
   (b) the Orient.
   (c) the West Indies.

4. Columbus' first voyage was paid for by
   (a) Queen Isabella.

(b) King Ferdinand.
(c) the Spanish Treasury.

5. The cost of Columbus' first voyage was
(a) $1,400.
(b) $14,000.
(c) $140,000.

6. Columbus' first voyage to the New World took
(a) three weeks.
(b) five weeks.
(c) two weeks.

7. Columbus named the island he first landed on
(a) San Salvador.
(b) the Canary Islands.
(c) the Bahamas.

8. The first settlers in the Western Hemisphere were looking for
(a) farmland.
(b) gold and jewels.
(c) slaves.

9. The first colony in the new land was called
(a) Haiti.
(b) the New World.
(c) Hispaniola.

10. During his last years, Columbus was
(a) given great honors.
(b) forgotten.
(c) very rich.

Vocabulary and Usage. Give the meaning of each of the following words. Use each in a sentence.

tribute	popularity
route	caravan
dwindle	pawn
compass	mutiny
optimistic	navigator

Conversation and Discussion. Why did the sailors want to turn back? What are some of the character traits that contemporary Americans admire about Columbus?

VII
Halloween

It was a brisk autumn evening. Mrs. Brown was sitting by the window, knitting. Suddenly, there was a sharp knock on her door, then two or three more knocks. Mrs. Brown heard whispers, giggles, and the rattling of paper. She opened the door a trifle, leaving the safety chain latched, and cautiously peered out through the crack. There stood three children wearing masks and costumes. When the children saw her, they shouted all together: "Trick or treat! Money or eats!"

"Well, what do you know!" Mrs. Brown said. "I'd forgotten. Tonight is Halloween. Let me see. I think I have some candy bars to give you." Each child carried a brown paper bag. Mrs. Brown dropped a candy bar into each bag. Then she said to one boy, who was holding a toy gun and wearing high boots, "What are you?"

"A cowboy, of course," he answered.

"I'm a ghost," shouted an even smaller child hidden under a white sheet.

"And I'm a skeleton," said the third child. "My bones glow in the dark." The "skeleton" was wearing a black suit with white bones painted on it.

"Thanks for the candy," shouted the children as they ran off to ring another doorbell.

"You're welcome," said Mrs. Brown. "Have fun. And don't play any pranks."

* * *

Every year on October 31, Halloween scenes like this occur throughout the United States. American children love to dress up in costumes and go "trick-or-treating." If an adult refuses to supply a treat—candy, cookies, fruit, or money—the children may play a trick. Typical Halloween pranks are soaping windows, writing on doors with crayons, overturning ashcans, and sticking pins into doorbells to keep them ringing.

Masquerading, begging, and many other Halloween customs are now mainly for the amusement of children. But hundreds of years ago these customs were performed quite seriously by adults as part of their religion.

In 835 A.D., the Roman Catholic Church declared November 1 a church holiday to honor all saints. The name *Halloween* is a short way of saying All Hallow's Eve, the night before All Saints' Day. *Hallow* means holy or sacred. But although Halloween gets its name from a Christian festival, its customs are of pagan origin. They come from two different sources: an ancient Celtic festival in honor of Samhain, lord of death, and a Roman festival in honor of Pomona, goddess of gardens and orchards. The Halloween colors, black and orange, suggest both ideas: death and harvest.

The "spooky" part of Halloween comes from the Celts, who occupied the British Isles and northern France during ancient and medieval times. The Celts worshiped gods of nature. They feared the coming of winter, associating it with death and evil spirits. Every year on October 31, the last day of the year on the old pagan calendar, the Druids (Celtic priests and teachers) built huge bonfires to scare away the demons of evil and death. They threw animals and crops from the harvest into the fire as gifts to appease the evil spirits. They dressed in ugly and frightening costumes so that the demons would think that they were one of them and do them no harm. Supposedly, on this evening ghosts rose from their graves and witches rode through the air on broomsticks or black cats. Also, the souls of dead relatives and friends were expected to return to earth for a visit. The Druid bonfires were built on hilltops to help guide these spirits back home.

From the Druid religion, then, come the custom of masquerading and the symbols of Halloween: ghosts, skeletons, devils, witches, black cats, and owls. The jack-o'-lantern is also of Celtic origin. It was an Irish custom to hollow out turnips and place lighted candles inside them to scare evil spirits away from the house. In the United States, the native pumpkin is used to make a jack-o'-lantern. First the pumpkin is hollowed out; then holes are cut in the shell to make the eyes, nose, and mouth. A candle is put inside, and the jack-o'-lantern is placed by the window.

The Irish also introduced the "trick-or-treat" custom hundreds of years ago. Groups of farmers would travel from house to house requesting food for the village's Halloween festivities. They would promise good luck to generous contributors and threaten those who were stingy.

Today American children go "trick-or-treating" not only for candy and other goodies, but also to collect money for such charitable organizations as UNICEF (United Nations Children's Fund).

The Druid holiday of Samhain contained many elements of a harvest festival. This part of the celebration became even more significant after 55 B.C. when the Romans invaded England and brought with them their harvest festival of Pomona. Thereafter, nuts and fruits —especially apples—became part of the Samhain ceremonies. Today at Halloween time, Americans honor the harvest by displaying cornstalks and pumpkins, eating nuts, autumn fruits, and pumpkin pies, and by playing games with apples. One of the most popular Halloween games is "bobbing for apples." In this game, apples float in a large tub of water. Each child tries to catch an apple in his mouth without using his hands to help.

The Druid religion lasted longest in Ireland and Scotland, and Halloween was most important in these two countries. In the late nineteenth century, Irish immigrants brought their Halloween customs to the United States. Today, Halloween is much more important in the United States than it is in Great Britain.

Many parents, schools, and community centers plan Halloween parties where children can have fun telling ghost stories, competing for prizes, bobbing for apples, and telling fortunes. Halloween, which began in ancient times as an evening of terror, is now an occasion of great merriment for youngsters. It is certainly one of the favorite holidays of American children.

EXERCISES

Comprehension. Choose the correct answer.

1. During Halloween night, children
   (a) sing songs.
   (b) play trick or treat.
   (c) stay at home.
2. Today, Halloween is a festival for
   (a) children.
   (b) adults.
   (c) religion.
3. Halloween was once part of
   (a) adult religious custom.
   (b) an Oriental religion.
   (c) a spring festival.
4. The name *Halloween* comes from
   (a) a pagan festival.
   (b) a Christian festival.
   (c) a Jewish festival.
5. Halloween gets its customs from
   (a) a pagan festival.
   (b) a Christian festival.
   (c) a Jewish festival.
6. The Druids were
   (a) Christian.
   (b) Roman.
   (c) Celtic.

7. The Druid religion lasted longest in
   (a) Germany and Italy.
   (b) Ireland and Scotland.
   (c) the United States.

8. The colors of Halloween are
   (a) red and green.
   (b) orange and black.
   (c) red, white, and blue.

9. In the United States, a jack-o'-lantern is made from
   (a) a turnip.
   (b) an apple.
   (c) a pumpkin.

10. Halloween customs were brought to the United States by
    (a) Italian immigrants.
    (b) Irish immigrants.
    (c) German immigrants.

Vocabulary and Usage. Give the meaning of each of the following words. Use each in a sentence.

festival	custom
harvest	symbol
costume	treat
ghost	trick
immigrant	appease

Conversation and Discussion. Describe the history of Halloween. Are there similar customs in other countries?

VIII
Thanksgiving

In the United States, the fourth Thursday in November is called Thanksgiving Day. On this day, Americans give thanks for the blessings they have enjoyed during the year. Thanksgiving is usually a family day, celebrated with big dinners and happy reunions.

The first American Thanksgiving was held in Plymouth, Massachusetts in 1621. The people of Plymouth had come to America from England in 1620. In their native land they had been called Puritans because they wished to "purify" the Church of England. Before 1600, some of them decided that they could not reform the Church from within, so they broke away and formed their own churches. When English officials began to persecute them, they fled to Holland.

Several years passed. The Puritans living in Holland were threatened by religious suppression and war and were saddened to see their children growing up Dutch instead of English. They wanted to keep their native language and traditions and to be free from religious persecution. Once again, they thought of moving. This time they considered America. In an unsettled land they would finally be free to live as they chose; and the idea of bringing the word of Christ to remote parts of the world appealed to them immensely. Some English merchants agreed to finance their journey in return for a share of the profits produced by the new colony. So, after traveling from Holland back to England, a small group of Puritans, together with some other passengers, set sail for the New World. The Puritans began to call themselves *Pilgrims* because of their wanderings in search of religious freedom.

It was September of 1620 when their ship, called the *Mayflower*, left port with 102 men, women, and children on board. This was the worst season of the year for an ocean crossing, and the trip was very rough. Yet, during the voyage, the travelers suffered only one death. Since there was also a birth aboard ship, the *Mayflower* was still carrying 102 passengers when, after sixty-five days at sea, she landed in Provincetown Harbor, inside the tip of Cape Cod, Massachusetts. The party had planned to land further south, nearer to the only other English colony in America, which was in Jamestown, Virginia. But errors in navigation and adverse winds brought the *Mayflower* to New England.

The Pilgrim leaders knew that they were in unsettled territory which had no governing body. They also knew that, in order to survive, every society needs a means of establishing and enforcing proper rules of conduct. Partly to protect themselves from rebels within their own ranks, forty-one men aboard the *Mayflower* held a meeting to choose their first governor and sign the historic Mayflower Compact, the first formal agreement for self-government in America.

For about a month longer, the Pilgrims lived aboard ship and sent out scouting parties to explore the coastline of Cape Cod Bay. At Plymouth, the scouts found a harbor with excellent fishing, some cleared land, cornfields, little rippling brooks with pure, fresh water, and a high hill that could be fortified. The site had once been an Indian village, but a smallpox epidemic a few years earlier had killed the entire Indian population. The scouts steered their small boat back to the *Mayflower* and reported their discovery. A few days later, the *Mayflower* sailed across Cape Cod Bay and anchored in Plymouth Harbor. Coming ashore in their small boat, the Pilgrims landed (according to tradition) on a large rock later named Plymouth Rock. This was the beginning of the second permanent English settlement in America.

The Pilgrims were poorly trained and poorly equipped to cope with life in the wilderness. During their first winter in the new land, they suffered tremendously. Poor food, hard work, infectious diseases, and bitterly cold weather killed about half of them. By the end of this terrible first winter, only about fifty Plymouth colonists remained alive.

One spring morning in 1621, an Indian walked into the little village of Plymouth and introduced himself in a friendly way. Later, he brought the Indian chief, Massasoit, who gave gifts to the Pilgrims and offered assistance. The Indians of Massasoit's tribe taught the Pilgrims how to hunt, fish, and grow food. They taught the Pilgrims to use fish for fertilizer in planting corn, pumpkins, and beans. Because of this help from the Indians, the Pilgrims had a good harvest.

Governor William Bradford was following an ancient tradition when, in the fall of 1621, he issued a proclamation establishing a day of thanksgiving to God. The Governor also decided to use this religious occasion to strengthen the bond of friendship between the Pilgrims and their Indian neighbors. So he invited Chief Massasoit and his braves to share the Thanksgiving feast.

The Indians gladly accepted and sent five deer ahead. The Pilgrim men went hunting and returned with turkey and other wild game. The women of Plymouth prepared delicious dishes from corn, cranberries, squash, and pumpkins.

The first Thanksgiving dinner was cooked and served out-of-doors. Although it was late autumn, huge fires kept the hosts and guests warm. Massasoit and ninety Indians joined the Pilgrims for the first Thanksgiving feast. The celebration lasted three days! On the first day, the Indians spent most of the time eating. On the second and third days, they wrestled, ran races, sang, and danced with the young people in Plymouth Colony. The holiday was a great success.

Many of the traditions of the modern American Thanksgiving come from that first Thanksgiving celebration more than 350 years ago. The modern Thanksgiving turkey is much like the ones that were hunted in the forests around Plymouth. Squash and corn, which were also harvested by the early Pilgrims, appear on the Thanksgiving table. Pumpkin pie and Indian pudding (a custard made from corn) are traditional Thanksgiving desserts.

The first Thanksgiving lasted three days. Today, for many Americans, it is a four-day holiday. Schools are closed on Thanksgiving Day and the day after. Many adults have both Thursday and Friday off from work. Relatives from other cities, students who have been away at school, and many other Americans travel long distances to spend the holiday at home.

Going home for Thanksgiving is a national custom, but every Thanksgiving about 10,000 Americans take a sentimental journey into early American history by visiting Plymouth, a modern city that reveres its past. In Plymouth Harbor, sightseers tour *Mayflower II*, a recently constructed ship similar to the original *Mayflower*. They see (but are not allowed to touch) the famous Plymouth Rock. Then they spend a few hours walking through a faithful reproduction of the original Pilgrim village as it looked in 1627. They enter the homes of famous colonists like Miles Standish and John Alden, and talk to the "residents" dressed in Pilgrim garb. The primitive living conditions reveal how very little the Pilgrims possessed in the way of material comforts. Modern Americans take great pride in these courageous forefathers who had so little by today's standards, but who were deeply thankful to God for giving them the things they valued most—a good harvest and the freedom to live and worship as they pleased. The half-million tourists who come to Plymouth every year find here a uniquely moving and inspiring experience.

A Famous Pilgrim Story

In 1858, Henry Wadsworth Longfellow, a famous American poet, wrote a long poem about the Pilgrims of

Plymouth Colony. It is called "The Courtship of Miles Standish."

Captain Miles Standish came to America with the Pilgrims, but he was not a Puritan and never joined the Pilgrim church. He was a trained soldier. It was his job to teach the men to fight enemies. The Captain was very brave in battle. Many times he saved the Pilgrims from being killed by hostile Indians.

Although he was a courageous warrior, Standish was timid with women. After his wife died, he was lonely and wanted to marry a lovely Puritan girl named Priscilla Mullens. But he was too shy to ask her. Instead, he begged his best friend, John Alden, to ask her for him.

Never were two friends so different. Standish was a short, stocky, middle-aged man. His red beard was already streaked with gray; his complexion was dark and rough. John Alden was a young man, fair-skinned, blond, and very handsome. Whereas Standish was a man of action, Alden was a scholar. In only one way were these two men alike: they both loved the same girl!

Poor John! He also loved Priscilla. But he wanted to be a loyal friend. Hiding his own feelings, he went to Priscilla and asked her to marry Miles Standish. He told her what a kind man the Captain was. He talked eloquently about Standish's bravery in battle and fine family background.

When John finished talking, Priscilla gave a surprising answer. Her reply is now very famous. She said, "Why don't you speak for yourself, John?"

John was too loyal to his friend to take Priscilla's advice. Instead, he returned to his friend and told him exactly what Priscilla had said. The Captain became very angry and shouted, "You have betrayed me!" A short time later, he left for an Indian campaign without saying good-bye to John.

While the Captain was gone, John and Priscilla saw each other often and grew to love each other more and more. However, John would not ask to marry her because he did not want to be an unfaithful friend. Only after a message arrived saying that Standish had been killed in battle did John propose marriage to Priscilla.

As the wedding ceremony ended, the guests were surprised and terrified to see a familiar figure standing in the doorway—a figure they thought was a ghost. It was Captain Miles Standish! He was dressed in armor, but he had not come to fight. He had come to apologize to his friend and beg forgiveness for his anger. At the end of the story, John, Priscilla, and Miles are united as friends.

EXERCISES

Comprehension. Choose the correct answer.

1. The first American Thanksgiving was hosted by
   (a) the Indians.
   (b) the Pilgrims.
   (c) the Spanish settlers.

2. The first group of English Puritans to land in America called themselves *Pilgrims* because
   (a) it was the name of their church.
   (b) they had wandered for a great distance in search of freedom.
   (c) they had been persecuted.

3. The Pilgrims came to America on a ship called the
   (a) *Mayflower*.
   (b) *Pinta*.
   (c) *Monitor*.

4. The Pilgrims were able to survive in America because
   (a) they received help from the Indians.
   (b) they were very rich.
   (c) many ships brought them food from England.
5. Thanksgiving was established in 1621 by Governor
   (a) Roger Williams.
   (b) William Bradford.
   (c) Miles Standish.
6. A traditional Pilgrim story often told at Thanksgiving concerns
   (a) Roger Williams.
   (b) William Bradford.
   (c) Miles Standish.
7. Both John Alden and Miles Standish
   (a) were soldiers.
   (b) loved Priscilla.
   (c) were scholars.
8. At first, John Alden asked Priscilla to marry
   (a) Standish.
   (b) Longfellow.
   (c) him.
9. Priscilla really loved
   (a) Miles Standish.
   (b) Longfellow.
   (c) John Alden.
10. At the end of the story, John, Miles, and Priscilla were
    (a) friends.
    (b) enemies.
    (c) angry.

Vocabulary and Usage. Give the meaning of each of the following words. Use each in a sentence.

reunion	purify
punish	persecute
ancient	delicious
hostile	timid
betray	scholar

Conversation and Discussion. Discuss the things in your own life for which you are thankful.

IX
Christmas and Hanukkah

CHRISTMAS

Christmas season is the most festive time of the year in the United States. Students from grammar school through college have one to two weeks' vacation, beginning shortly before Christmas and ending soon after New Year's. Many families go away for the holidays, perhaps to ski in Colorado or to swim and sunbathe in Florida. Those who stay home have fun, too. There are numerous parties to celebrate the birth of Christ and the arrival of the new year.

Although no one knows exactly when Jesus was born, Christians throughout the world celebrate His birthday on December 25. This date was selected in the fourth century so that Christmas would replace the pagan celebration of the winter solstice. Ancient peoples believed that daylight hours began to lengthen when the sun god started his journey back to earth. They celebrated the beginning of his journey on December 25.

In the United States, the spirit of Christmas arrives about a month before the holiday itself. Late in November, street lights and store windows are decorated with the traditional Christmas colors of red and green. Snowmen, Santa Claus, shepherds, angels, and Nativity scenes appear in countless shop windows. Fir trees, holly wreaths, and mistletoe are familiar sights. Families decorate their homes, inside and out, with colored lights and evergreens.

The manufacture and distribution of Christmas items is big business. Stores depend upon Christmas shoppers for about one-fourth of their annual sales. Smart shoppers buy their gifts in November or early December, before the "Christmas rush" makes shopping a chore. Christmas is expensive. To earn extra money for gifts, thousands of Americans get part-time jobs during December delivering mail or selling gifts, trees, ornaments, or greeting cards. Many people make monthly bank deposits in special Christmas accounts so that they will have enough money to provide a nice Christmas for their families.

Although Americans enjoy the commercial gaiety of Christmas, the most beautiful and meaningful aspects of the holiday occur at home and in church. Many families go to church on Christmas Eve and Christmas morning. After services, they gather around the tree and open their gifts. Then they sit down to enjoy a traditional Christmas dinner—turkey or ham, sweet potatoes, vegetables, cranberry sauce, and nuts. For dessert, there is usually fruit cake, plum pudding, or mince pie.

Most of the Christmas customs which Americans enjoy today are variations of traditions brought here by European immigrants. These are some of the most popular customs:

Exchanging Gifts. The first Christmas gifts were those that the three Wise Men brought to the infant Jesus. The custom of giving gifts to family members and close friends is extremely popular in the United States today. Both children and adults get Christmas presents, although children usually get many more.

Receiving Toys from Santa Claus. Many American children believe that on Christmas Eve Santa Claus, a fat, jolly man who wears a red suit, red hat, and long white beard, slides down their chimney to bring them gifts. According to the story, Santa Claus travels in a sleigh pulled by eight reindeer. Children tell Santa Claus what toys they want by writing him a letter or visiting him in a local department store. On Christmas Eve many youngsters lie awake listening for Santa and his sleigh. Some children even leave him a snack of milk and cookies.

Santa Claus is the American name for St. Nicholas, a generous fourth-century bishop who lived in what is now Turkey. It was his custom to go out at night and bring gifts to the needy. After his death, his fame spread throughout Europe. During the Middle Ages, he became the patron saint of schoolboys. His feast day (December 6) was once celebrated in many European countries and is still celebrated in some. Dutch immigrants brought the concept of St. Nicholas (whom they called *Sinter Klaas*) to America, where the name was mispronounced and finally changed to *Santa Claus*. Nineteenth-century American artists and authors altered St. Nick's appearance and created the roly-poly man in red that we see today. Santa's sleigh and reindeer were derived from an old Norse legend.

The American version of Santa Claus as a person who brings gifts and goodwill at Christmastime has also become popular in Canada, England, and Australia.

Hanging a Stocking near the Chimney. As in Great Britain, American children hang stockings by the fireplace, hoping that Santa will fill them with candy and toys.

Decorating the Home with Evergreens. The winter custom of decorating homes and churches with evergreens began in ancient times. Branches of fir or spruce were thought to bring good luck and guarantee the return of spring. The early Germans believed, for example, that in winter evil spirits killed the plants and trees and caused green leaves and flowers to disappear. They felt that bringing evergreens into their homes would protect them from the spirit of death.

Germans of the sixteenth century probably originated the custom of decorating trees. In the nineteenth century, the idea spread throughout Europe and the United States. Now, at Christmastime decorated trees stand in about two-thirds of American homes. The modern American tree is usually covered with colored balls and strings of colored lights. The star on top represents the star in the East which guided the three Wise Men to Bethlehem.

In ancient times, a branch of mistletoe was hung over

doorways for good luck. Today the custom continues, but now it is for fun. A man may kiss any girl he catches standing under the mistletoe.

The poinsettia plant is another familiar Christmas decoration. Its star-shaped red leaves are an ideal symbol of the holiday. This plant is native to Central America and Mexico. In the nineteenth century it was adapted to cultivation in the United States by Dr. Poinsett of South Carolina. It is a distinctly modern and American Christmas tradition.

Singing Christmas Carols. In the early days of the Christian Church, the bishops sang carols on Christmas Day. Now, everybody sings them. Soloists and choirs on the radio, on TV, in church, and in school all help fill the winter air with beautiful music. Copying an old English custom, many Americans join with friends and walk from house to house singing the traditional carols of Christmas.

Sending Christmas Cards. The custom of sending Christmas cards began in London in 1843 and came to the United States in 1875. Today, most Americans (Christians and non-Christians) send dozens of Christmas cards or "season's greetings" to relatives, friends, and business associates.

HANUKKAH

While Christians brighten the winter scene with Christmas color and lights, American Jews (together with Jews throughout the world) celebrate their Feast of Lights—Hanukkah. This holiday commemorates a triumph of religious freedom. In 168 B.C., the Syrian King Antiochus conquered Judea and tried to force the Jews to worship pagan gods. Three years later, a small band of Jews led by Judas Maccabaeus defeated the powerful Syrian armies.

When the Jews recaptured Jerusalem and rededicated their Holy Temple, they relit the eternal lamp. One day's supply of oil—all that was left—burned for eight days, until fresh oil was available. In memory of this miracle, Jews celebrate Hanukkah for eight days and light candles in a special candleholder called a *menorah.* In addition to the candle used to light the others, Jews light one candle on the first day of Hanukkah, two on the second day, and so on until the eighth day, when candles are burning in all nine branches of the *menorah.*

The date of Hanukkah is determined by the Hebrew calendar, but the holiday always occurs in December. So, for Americans of both Christian and Jewish faiths, the year ends in a spirit of joy and reverence.

EXERCISES

Comprehension. Choose the correct answer.

1. Christmas replaced the pagan celebration of the
   (a) harvest festival.
   (b) spring planting.
   (c) winter solstice.

2. The first Christmas gifts were given by
   (a) the three Wise Men.
   (b) Judas Maccabaeus.
   (c) King Antiochus.

3. Which of the following Christmas traditions came from Germany?
   (a) the Christmas tree.
   (b) exchanging gifts.
   (c) Santa Claus.

4. Which of the following Christmas traditions came from England?
   (a) the Christmas tree.
   (b) the poinsettia.
   (c) Christmas cards.

5. Which of the following Christmas traditions began in America?
   (a) the poinsettia plant.
   (b) Christmas caroling.
   (c) mistletoe.

6. In 168 B.C., Judea was conquered by
   (a) Judas Maccabaeus.
   (b) the Syrian King Antiochus.
   (c) Hanukkah.

7. In 165 B.C., Judea was freed by
   (a) Judas Maccabaeus.
   (b) the Syrian King Antiochus.
   (c) Hanukkah.

8. When the Jews relit the Temple's lamp, one day's supply of oil burned for

(a) four days.
(b) six days.
(c) eight days.

9. Hanukkah celebrates
   (a) the birth of a great leader.
   (b) a triumph of religious liberty.
   (c) a victory against Rome.

10. The traditional candleholder of Hanukkah is called a
    (a) calendar.
    (b) menorah.
    (c) lamp.

Vocabulary and Usage. Give the meaning of each of the following words. Use each in a sentence.

festive	decorate
chore	legend
luck	cultivation
distinct	worship
triumph	conquer

Conversation and Discussion. Many different Christmas traditions are observed around the world. Discuss some of the differences between Christmas as celebrated in the United States and Christmas as celebrated in other countries.

X
New Year's Celebrations

"Ring out the old, ring in the new," wrote Alfred Lord Tennyson, the nineteenth-century English poet. And that's exactly what Americans do every December 31. New Year's Eve is a time for merriment. At midnight, bells ring, horns blow, and friends exchange kisses. Everyone stays up late to celebrate the arrival of another new year.

At home or in restaurants, most Americans spend the

final hours of the old year and the first hours of the new year drinking and dining with friends. One popular New Year's Eve drink is eggnog, a thick, yellow concoction made with eggs, milk or cream, and sugar. Throughout the Christmas season, eggnog mixed with rum or brandy is a familiar party beverage. Champagne—the drink that traditionally symbolizes a celebration—is often served for the midnight toast on New Year's Eve.

One of the noisiest and most crowded of New Year's Eve celebrations takes place in New York City at Times Square. Thousands of New Yorkers gather there, and millions of Americans across the country join them via TV. The new year arrives earlier on the East Coast than in other parts of the country because the United States spans four time zones. When midnight comes to New York, it is 11 P.M. in Chicago, 10 P.M. in Denver, and only 9 P.M. in Los Angeles.

After the new year officially arrives, most party-goers enjoy a hearty snack. New Year's Eve festivities often continue until two or three o'clock in the morning. Many people travel from one party to another to celebrate with several different groups of friends.

Following a long, hectic New Year's Eve, Americans spend a quiet, leisurely New Year's Day. In most households, everyone sleeps late, then enjoys brunch and TV with the family and friends. Two picturesque New Year's Day festivals receive widespread attention and coverage by the news media: the Mummer's Parade and the Tournament of Roses. Both these events have been American traditions for more than half a century.

The Mummer's Parade, which takes place in Philadelphia, is a ten-hour spectacle that usually attracts more than a million spectators. The idea is based upon a custom brought to the United States in the mid-1600s and practiced by Swedish and English immigrants who settled along the Delaware River. The men used to welcome the new year by roaming the countryside in costume. Today, the Mummer's Parade is more orderly but still colorful and high-spirited. The men dress in lavish costumes. Some impersonate women since no women are allowed to participate. There are clowns, musicians, dancers, and floats—altogether about 17,000 marchers led by King Momus dressed in gleaming satin.

The Tournament of Roses takes place in Pasadena, California. Elaborate floats displaying roses and thousands of other California flowers depict a different theme each year. Prizes are awarded for the most unusual and attractive floral displays. After the parade, the Rose Bowl football game, a contest between two top-ranking college football teams, is played.

The Mummer's Parade, the Tournament of Roses, and the Rose Bowl game attract thousands of tourists and millions of TV viewers. Meanwhile, in different parts of the country, other "bowl" games attract national attention and TV coverage. All these events help to make January 1 an entertaining and relaxing holiday.

New Year's Day has traditionally been the occasion for starting new programs and giving up bad habits. People talk about "turning over a new leaf." Many Americans make New Year's resolutions, promising to improve their behavior. Typical New Year's resolutions are to spend less money, give up smoking, begin a diet, or control one's temper.

From ancient times to the present, New Year's customs have been connected with saying farewell to the past and looking forward to a better future. Although the theme of the holiday has not altered much from one century to the next, the date of the celebration has been changed many times. The ancient Egyptians launched their year on September 21, while the ancient Greeks began theirs on June 21. The old Roman calendar contained only ten months, and New Year's Day was March 1. In 46 B.C. Julius Caesar introduced an improved calendar containing two additional months, January and February. January was named for the Roman god Janus, whose name comes from the Roman word for *door*. Like a door, Janus looks both ways; he is usually depicted with two faces, one looking backward and the other forward. Julius Caesar's calendar, called in his honor the *Julian* calendar, was revised in 1582 by Pope Gregory XIII. The *Gregorian* calendar is the one in use today.

All Americans celebrate New Year's on December 31 and January 1, but Chinese-Americans and Jewish-Americans also celebrate their own special new year holidays. Although the Chinese have officially adopted the Gregorian calendar, many still celebrate the New Year holiday established by China's ancient lunar calendar more than 4,000 years ago.

The fifteen-day Chinese New Year begins with *Yuan Tan* and concludes with the Festival of Lanterns, held at the time of the full moon. Yuan Tan, which falls between January 21 and February 19, is a solemn family holiday highlighted by prayers and feasting. During the next two weeks, a joyous spirit prevails. Friends and relatives visit one another, exchanging baskets of fruit and other gifts. There are parades featuring musicians, clowns, acrobats, stilt-walkers, and dancers. The New Year celebration ends with the beautiful Festival of Lanterns. Paper and glass lanterns in assorted shapes and sizes are strung on porches, along the streets, and in front of temples. A lantern parade is led by a bamboo dragon, symbol of goodness and strength.

There are more than 435,000 Chinese-Americans, and almost all of them live in urban areas. Therefore, in many American cities there are Chinese New Year celebrations. The most elaborate displays are in New York and San Francisco. Lavish parades usually include a huge replica of a Buddhist lion, a block-long golden dragon, dozens of floats, and marching bands. Thousands of spectators come to view these splendid exhibitions.

Rosh Hashanah (which means *head of the year*) is the traditional Jewish New Year. It occurs in September or October. Unlike the American New Year, Rosh Hashanah is a very solemn holiday, marking the beginning of ten days of penitence called the High Holy Days. These days are set aside for self-appraisal, repentance, and the making of vows to be a better person in the coming year.

The climax and conclusion of the High Holy Days is *Yom Kippur*, the Day of Atonement. This is the holiest day of the Jewish year. Religious Jews fast from sundown on the eve of Yom Kippur until sundown of the following day. They spend most of this period in prayer at the synagogue. At the conclusion of Yom Kippur services, God's symbolic book of deeds and judgments is closed for the year.

* * *

To Americans of all races, religions, and national origins, the closing of one calendar year and the opening of another is a serious, yet happy occasion. We review the past with nostalgia. We judge ourselves and promise to improve. And we look forward to a new beginning with renewed hope.

EXERCISES

Comprehension. Choose the correct answer.

1. The New Year's Eve celebration is usually a
   (a) religious holiday.
   (b) social event.
   (c) family party.

2. New Year's Day is usually spent
   (a) with the family.
   (b) at a party.
   (c) as an ordinary working day.

3. The Mummer's Parade takes place in
   (a) Philadelphia.
   (b) New York.
   (c) Pasadena.

4. The Tournament of Roses takes place in
   (a) Philadelphia.
   (b) New York.
   (c) Pasadena.

5. The calendar which determines the time of the Christian New Year is called
   (a) the Julian calendar.
   (b) the Gregorian calendar.
   (c) the Koranic calendar.

6. The Chinese New Year begins with
   (a) Yom Kippur.
   (b) Yuan Tan.
   (c) Rosh Hashanah.

7. The traditional Chinese New Year celebration concludes with a feast called
   (a) the Festival of Lanterns.
   (b) Janus.
   (c) the Feast of Lights.

8. Most Chinese-Americans live in
   (a) urban centers.
   (b) rural areas.
   (c) Chicago.

9. The Jewish New Year is called
   (a) Rosh Hashanah.
   (b) Yuan Tan.
   (c) Hanukkah.

10. The Jewish High Holy Days conclude with
   (a) Rosh Hashanah.
   (b) Yom Kippur.
   (c) Yuan Tan.

Vocabulary and Usage. Give the meaning of each of the following words. Use each in a sentence.

merriment	concoction
span	impersonate
resolution	parade
elaborate	replica
splendid	penitence

Conversation and Discussion. Make a list of New Year's resolutions. Discuss what you should do during the new year.

XI
Holidays Honoring Two Great Presidents

Most Americans celebrate the birthdays of George Washington and Abraham Lincoln as legal holidays. Why are these two presidents especially honored? Both of them lived during critical periods in American history, and both met the challenge of their times with courage and wisdom. Washington helped bring the United States into existence, and Lincoln kept the young nation from splitting in two. The determination and foresight of these great leaders helped to create the strong and independent country that exists today.

But Washington and Lincoln are remembered not only for their political accomplishments. Both men are American heroes, symbols of traits and ideals which are much admired by the nation they helped to build.

GEORGE WASHINGTON

George Washington, the "father of his country," was born in 1732. The son of a wealthy Virginia planter, he was privately educated and trained to be a surveyor. But as an officer in the French and Indian War he became interested in military leadership.

In 1759, Washington married a widow named Martha Custis, who was later to become famous as a gracious hostess in the first President's home. After his marriage, he returned to his Virginia plantation, Mt. Vernon, to live the life of a gentleman farmer. He also became involved in colonial opposition to British policies in America.

By 1775, relations with England had grown so bad that the colonists were ready to fight for their independence. The Continental Congress appointed Washington commander-in-chief of the revolutionary forces. His job was incredibly difficult. His army was meager in size, ill-fed, and inadequately clothed. The men suffered greatly during terribly cold winters. While begging for more men and supplies, Washington had to fight the Revolutionary War with poorly equipped, untrained soldiers. He never asked for and never received any salary for the job he performed. In fact, he often spent his own money to buy clothing for his men and send aid to their families. Washington brought to the battlefield great military ability, perseverance, staunch patriotism, and a noble character.

Washington was the first man not a king whose birthday was publicly celebrated during his lifetime. Before the colonies declared their independence, festivities honoring the birthdays of British rulers were customary. After the Declaration of Independence, the American people ignored royal birthdays and began instead to celebrate General Washington's birthday. This custom started in 1778 during the army's harsh winter at Valley Forge, when one of the artillery bands marched to Washington's headquarters and serenaded him.

When the war ended in 1783, Washington eagerly returned to Mt. Vernon. But his peaceful retirement was interrupted when he was unanimously chosen first President of the United States. He took office in 1789 and was reelected in 1792. In 1796, he declined a third term and retired from political life. He died two years later and was buried at Mt. Vernon, a dignified and lovely estate which a million tourists visit every year. Shortly after his death, Washington was eulogized in these famous words: "First in war, first in peace, and first in the hearts of his countrymen."

To the American people, Washington symbolizes dignity, statesmanship, and, above all, honesty. The famous cherry tree story, which was invented by Washington's first biographer, has become a lesson in morals for all American school children. The story goes like this: When George Washington was about six years old, his father gave him a hatchet, which the little boy loved to play with. One day, he tried the edge of his hatchet on his father's favorite young cherry tree and did enough damage to kill the tree. Next morning, his father noticed the damage and ran into the house shouting, "George, do you know who killed that beautiful little cherry tree yonder in the garden?"

George's famous reply was, "I can't tell a lie, Pa, you know I can't tell a lie. I did cut it with my hatchet." His father, impressed by the boy's courage and honesty, quickly forgave him. Because of this fictitious tale, traditional desserts on Washington's Birthday are cherry pie or a log-shaped cake decorated with chocolate icing and cherries. In most states, the holiday is now celebrated on the third Monday in February.

ABRAHAM LINCOLN

Much as Americans admire George Washington, the greatest of all American heroes is certainly Abraham Lincoln. Why? Basic to the American philosophy is the idea that an individual with ability, perseverance, and strength of character can achieve success no matter how humble his beginnings. Lincoln is a classic example of the self-made man.

Lincoln was born on February 12, 1809 in a log cabin in Kentucky. His parents were uneducated and poor. Although Lincoln eventually became a lawyer, he had very little formal schooling. But he did possess a brilliant mind and great moral strength. He had the courage to do what he felt was right, no matter what the sacrifice. In 1860, shortly before the Civil War began, he said, "Let us have faith that right makes might; and in that faith let us to the end, dare to do our duty as we understand it."

Elected to the presidency in 1860 and reelected in 1864, Lincoln was the first successful presidential candidate nominated by the Republican Party. During his term in office, the American Civil War was fought. The issues were slavery and secession. In the agricultural southern states, Negro slaves forcibly brought from Africa were used to cultivate tobacco and cotton and do housework. In the industrial North, where there were only small farms,

the economy had little use for large masses of agricultural laborers. Northerners disapproved of slavery as being inhumane. In order to protect their right to keep slaves, the southern leaders decided that the southern states should secede from the Union and form a separate nation—the Confederate States of America.

Lincoln felt that the Union must be preserved. In 1860, the United States was the only important democracy in the world. Self-government would be proved a failure if the nation could be destroyed by a minority of its own citizens. Lincoln chose to lead the country into civil war rather than allow the South to secede.

In 1858, Lincoln had said, "A house divided against

itself cannot stand. I believe this government cannot endure permanently half slave and half free." In keeping with his belief, Lincoln issued the Emancipation Proclamation in 1863, declaring all slaves in the rebellious states to be free. After the Civil War, the Thirteenth Amendment to the Constitution was adopted. This amendment freed all slaves throughout the nation.

Because he was a masterful writer who could express his beliefs clearly and with great emotional force, Lincoln was able to make Northerners understand why they were fighting a bloody civil war. Portions of his speeches are still memorized by schoolchildren because they express in stirring language the highest ideals of American democracy.

In 1863, in dedicating a national cemetery in Gettysburg, Pennsylvania, he concluded his shortest and most famous address with the following wish: ". . . that this nation, under God, shall have a new birth of freedom, and that government of the people, by the people, for the people shall not perish from the earth."

On April 14, 1865, less than a week after the Civil War ended, Lincoln attended a theatrical performance at Ford's Theatre in Washington, D.C. Shortly after 10 P.M., a gunshot rang through the crowded auditorium. John Wilkes Booth, a well-known actor and Southern sympathizer, had shot the President in the head. Lincoln was carried unconscious to a neighboring house, where he died early the following morning.

Because he had spent most of his adult years in Illinois, Lincoln's body was brought back to his home state and buried in Springfield. Now there is a huge monument above the spot where Lincoln, his wife, and three of their four sons are buried.

Lincoln's Birthday is not celebrated in the South. The twenty-six states that do observe the holiday celebrate it either on February 12 or on the first Monday in February.

* * *

In Washington, D.C., beautiful monuments have been dedicated to Washington and Lincoln. Every year the tourists who see these magnificent structures recall the courage and nobility of these great American presidents.

EXERCISES

Comprehension. Choose the correct answer.

1. George Washington is known to Americans as
   (a) the father of his country.
   (b) the President of the Continental Congress.
   (c) the author of the Declaration of Independence.

2. Washington's first office in the cause of the colonies was as
   (a) President of the United States.
   (b) commander-in-chief of the Army.
   (c) Secretary of State.

3. After the Revolutionary War ended, Washington returned to
   (a) Mt. Vernon.
   (b) New York.
   (c) Illinois.

4. As President, Washington served
   (a) one term.
   (b) two terms.
   (c) three terms.

5. Washington is buried
   (a) at Mount Vernon.
   (b) in New York.
   (c) in Illinois.

6. Abraham Lincoln was born
   (a) into a wealthy family.
   (b) in Washington.
   (c) in poor surroundings.

7. Lincoln was a member of the
   (a) Democratic Party.
   (b) Republican Party.
   (c) Populist Party.

8. Lincoln was first elected President in
   (a) 1910.
   (b) 1789.
   (c) 1860.

9. The principal issues of the Civil War were
   (a) emancipation of women.
   (b) slavery and secession.
   (c) cotton and tobacco.

10. Shortly after the Civil War, Lincoln was
   (a) assassinated.
   (b) reelected.
   (c) married.

Vocabulary and Usage. Give the meaning of each of the following words. Use each in a sentence.

critical	wisdom
meager	perseverance
assassinate	revolution
sympathize	nobility
eulogize	monument

Conversation and Discussion. What might the United States be like today if either Washington or Lincoln had not appeared at such critical times?

XII
Minor Holidays

From February through June, Americans celebrate five minor holidays which are important because of the light-hearted enjoyment they bring. These are not legal holidays. When they occur on weekdays, schools and businesses stay open as usual. But these occasions involve customs which are bright threads in the fabric of American culture.

St. Valentine's Day is a festival of romance and affection. This holiday is another interesting blend of pagan and Christian influences. Some of the day's customs probably come from an ancient Roman holiday called Lupercalia, a celebration which honored Juno (the goddess of women, marriage, and childbirth) and Pan (the god of nature). During the Middle Ages, church leaders wished to relate this popular holiday to Christianity, so they renamed it after one or both third-century Christian martyrs named Valentine and shifted the date from February 15 to the feast day of St. Valentine, February 14. There seems to be no logical reason why St. Valentine should have become the patron saint of lovers, except perhaps for a medieval European belief that birds began to mate on February 14.

Shortly before February 14, card shops, bookstores, department stores, and drugstores display a wide assortment of greeting cards called *valentines*. Most valentines are illustrated with the symbolic red heart; many show a picture of Cupid with his bow and arrow. Some are very fancy—decorated with paper lace, scented satin, feathers, ribbons, or bows—and contain tender verses. The plainer ones say simply, "Be my Valentine." There are special valentines with messages directed to specific family members. For sweethearts and friends, there are valentines in every imaginable style—sentimental, restrained, sophisticated, humorous, or insulting.

Valentines may cost anywhere from a penny to more than a dollar, depending upon the size and degree of decoration. Grammar school children usually buy packages of small, inexpensive valentines to give to classmates and teachers. Sweethearts and married couples may exchange more expensive ones, along with small gifts. Men often give flowers or candy (in a red, heart-shaped box) for a Valentine's Day gift.

The custom of sending written valentines began in Europe around 1400. It was brought to this country by the earliest English settlers. Today, Americans probably send more valentines than people in all other countries put together. Our annual sale of valentines is more than 550 million!

St. Patrick's Day honors Ireland's patron saint, the beloved religious leader who, in the latter part of the fourth century, brought Christianity to a pagan nation. Americans of Irish descent celebrate the anniversary of his death on March 17.

Strangely enough, the patron saint of Ireland was not Irish either by birth or heritage. Born in what is now Scotland or England, he was the son of Roman citizens. When he was sixteen years old, he was captured by pirates and brought to Ireland, where he was sold as a slave. He spent six years in bondage in Ireland. During this time he observed the Irish worshiping idols and dreamed that he was destined to bring Christianity to them. When he escaped, he went to France, where he studied religion and later became a monk. He eventually returned to Ireland, where he preached Christianity and established more than 300 churches.

St. Patrick is the favorite saint of the Irish, who tell many stories about his kind deeds and miraculous powers. He is even given credit for driving the snakes out of Ireland!

In the United States, St. Patrick's Day is celebrated by parades, church services, banquets, and "the wearing of the green," the color which symbolizes the south of Ireland. Green cloth shamrocks (three-leaf clovers which St. Patrick used to explain the Trinity and which have now come to symbolize the Irish nation) are sold on the streets and worn by millions on this day.

In New York City, Boston, Philadelphia, and Atlanta (all cities with large Irish populations), there are spectacular St. Patrick's Day parades. The women wear native Irish costumes. The men carry colorful banners and flags. Bands play familiar songs about Ireland, and observers, crowding the sidewalks to watch the fun, sing or hum along with the marchers. In Chicago, there is also a St. Patrick's Day parade, and, as part of the festivities, the Chicago River is dyed green!

April Fool's Day is the first day of April. The sport of the holiday is to play silly but harmless jokes on family members, co-workers, and friends. A victim of one of these pranks is called an *April fool.*

This holiday originated in France. When the French first adopted the Gregorian calendar in 1564, some people continued to use the old calendar and to celebrate New Year's Day on April 1. These people were called April fools. The custom of playing tricks on this day became popular in France and then spread to many other countries. April Fool's jokes are as ingenious, humorous, or cruel as the people who perform them. Here are some typical pranks:

— Calling the zoo and asking to speak to Mr. Lion.
— Putting salt in the sugar bowl.
— Setting the clocks back an hour.
— Saying to a friend, "Oh my. You have four big holes in your coat—buttonholes."
— Tying a string to a wallet and leaving the wallet in the middle of the sidewalk. When someone stoops to pick it up, the prankster yanks it out of reach.

In the United States today, April Fool's jokes are played

mostly by children, who enjoy the holiday immensely.

Mother's Day is celebrated on the second Sunday in May. On this occasion, Mother usually receives greeting cards and gifts from her husband and children. For most mothers, the rarest and best gift is a day of rest. Often, families honor Mother by taking her out for dinner. In some households the husband and children take over meal preparations so that Mom can spend a whole day away from the kitchen. Serving her breakfast in bed is another family ritual. Later in the day, parents may take their children to visit their grandparents.

Flowers are an important part of the holiday. Mothers are often given corsages for the occasion, particularly if they are elderly.

The idea of setting aside a special day to honor mothers did not originate in the United States. In England, Mothering Sunday, celebrated during Lent, was once traditional. The Yugoslavs and many other peoples have long observed a holiday for mothers. In the United States, Mother's Day has been a national tradition since 1915.

Father's Day is celebrated throughout the United States and Canada on the third Sunday in June. The holiday customs are similar to Mother's Day. Dad also receives greeting cards and gifts from his family and enjoys a day of leisure.

EXERCISES

Comprehension. Choose the correct answer.

1. St. Valentine's Day is
   (a) in honor of Ireland's patron saint.
   (b) in honor of all mothers.
   (c) a festival of romance.

2. On February 14, people exchange
   (a) green cloth shamrocks.
   (b) valentines.
   (c) jokes.

3. St. Patrick's Day honors
   (a) Ireland's patron saint.
   (b) all mothers.
   (c) shamrocks.

4. St. Patrick's Day is celebrated by
   (a) parades.
   (b) cards.
   (c) jokes.

5. St. Patrick first went to Ireland as a
   (a) preacher.
   (b) teacher.
   (c) slave.

6. April Fool's Day falls on
   (a) April 1.
   (b) April 15.
   (c) April 30.

7. April Fool's Day originated in
   (a) Ireland.
   (b) France.
   (c) England.

8. Mother's Day is celebrated in
   (a) May.
   (b) March.
   (c) April.

9. In the United States, Mother's Day has been a national tradition since
   (a) 1860.
   (b) 1776.
   (c) 1915.

10. Father's Day is celebrated in
    (a) May.
    (b) April.
    (c) June.

Vocabulary and Usage. Give the meaning of each of the following words. Use each in a sentence.

romance	affection
card	saint
parade	joke
prank	honor
rare	ritual

Conversation and Discussion. Describe some of the minor holidays of other countries.

XIII
Easter and Related Holidays

Although the Christian religion gave the world Easter as we know it today, the celebration owes its name and many of its customs and symbols to a pagan festival called Eostre. Eostre, the Anglo-Saxon goddess of springtime and sunrise, got her name from the word *east*, where the sun rises. Every spring northern European peoples celebrated the festival of Eostre to honor the awakening of new life in nature. Christians related the rising of the sun to the resurrection of Jesus and their own spiritual rebirth.

The Crucifixion did, of course, historically occur in the spring. The Last Supper, which took place on a Thursday, the day before the Crucifixion, was a traditional Jewish *Passover* feast. The early Christians celebrated Easter on the same date as Passover. But they were dissatisfied with this date because they wanted Easter to fall on a Sunday every year, and Passover did not. For some time, Easter was celebrated on different dates in different places. Finally, in 325 A.D. a council of churchmen solved the problem with the help of astronomers. They decided that Easter should be celebrated on the Sunday following the first full moon after March 21. The full moon was important because, many years ago, it helped to guide travelers who wished to join friends and relatives at big Easter festivals.

Many modern Easter symbols come from pagan times. The egg, for instance, was a fertility symbol long before the Christian era. The ancient Persians, Greeks, and Chinese exchanged eggs at their spring festivals. In Christian times the egg took on a new meaning, symbolizing the tomb from which Christ rose. The ancient custom of dyeing eggs at Easter time is still very popular with American children.

The Easter bunny also originated in pre-Christian fertility lore. The rabbit was the most fertile animal our ancestors knew, so they selected it as a symbol of new life. Today, children enjoy eating candy bunnies and listening to stories about the Easter bunny, who supposedly brings Easter eggs in a fancy basket.

Traditionally, the meats associated with Easter are lamb and ham. Both of these meats have had symbolic meaning since ancient times. In the Old Testament, Abraham used the ram as a sacrifice after God ordered him not to kill his son Isaac. The sacrificial lamb has always been a part of the Passover tradition. For Christians, the lamb symbolizes the sacrifice of Christ. For thousands of years the pig has been a symbol of good luck. On Easter Sunday, smoked or cooked ham is the traditional main course in both Europe and the United States.

Easter is a time for rejoicing. The continual rebirth of physical life on earth symbolizes the eternity of spiritual life. But the deeper significance of Easter lies in a profound paradox. The story of Christ implies that for all Christians the source of eternal life is physical death.

Christians observe several holidays in remembrance of the last days of Christ and His Crucifixion:

Shrovetide is the English name for the three or four days preceding Lent. Years ago, when Lenten restrictions were far more rigorous than they are today, Shrovetide was celebrated everywhere by parties, games, dances, and feasting. It is still carnival season in many European countries.

The last day of Shrovetide is called Shrove Tuesday or *Mardi Gras* (French for Fat Tuesday). In the United States, a few southern cities have elaborate *Mardi Gras* celebrations. The most famous one occurs in New Orleans, Louisiana. The New Orleans *Mardi Gras* lasts six days and features torchlight parades, beautiful floats, marching bands, and masked costume balls. Thousands of tourists come to see this event.

Lent begins with Ash Wednesday. On this day, when a Catholic approaches the church altar, the priest makes the sign of the cross on his forehead with penitential ashes. Lent extends for forty weekdays before Easter Sunday. It honors the forty days that Jesus spent alone in the desert, fasting and praying.

Palm Sunday, the beginning of Holy Week, commemorates the day that Jesus rode into Jerusalem on a donkey, with the people cheering and spreading palm branches on the path before Him.

Maundy Thursday (Holy Thursday) comes three days before Easter. It is in remembrance of Christ's Last Supper with His disciples. Maundy means a command. At the Last Supper, Jesus commanded his disciples to love one another.

Good Friday, the saddest of Christian holidays, recalls the Friday of the Crucifixion. It is a day of penitence and mourning. The name is probably a corruption of God's Friday. Current American Good Friday customs include eating hot cross buns (spiced rolls decorated with the mark of the cross) and attending church services.

Easter Sunday begins early for many American families. Many people attend sunrise services, a custom brought to this country by European settlers. Easter is a family day. After services, relatives get together for large Easter dinners.

It is an almost universal custom to put on new clothes at Easter—a whole new outfit or at least a new hat or new pair of gloves. This custom predates Christianity, originating in pagan spring festivals. It also reflects the early Christian custom of new white Easter robes for the newly baptized. Now many American cities have Easter parades. People enjoy the return of milder weather by walking outdoors to display their new spring clothes.

PASSOVER

Passover, the festival which Jesus was celebrating at the Last Supper, is still one of the most important Jewish holidays. It is a tribute to freedom, commemorating the liberation of the Hebrews from slavery in ancient Egypt.

According to the Book of Exodus, almost four thousand years ago the Hebrews were kept in bondage in Egypt. The men were used as workers to build great Egyptian monuments. When Moses asked Pharaoh, the ruler of Egypt, to let the Hebrews make a religious pilgrimage, Pharaoh refused. For this refusal, God punished Egypt with a series of horrible plagues. The last and worst plague was the death of every Egyptian firstborn. The Hebrews escaped this punishment by sprinkling their doorposts with the blood of a lamb. The Angel of Death "passed over" households so marked. Thus, the holiday is called *Passover*.

After this final plague, Pharaoh agreed to release the Hebrews. Then he changed his mind and sent his soldiers after them. Another miracle—the parting of the Red Sea—allowed the Hebrews to escape from their Egyptian pursuers.

While preparing to flee from Egypt, the Hebrews ate flat, unleavened slabs of bread (called *matzos*) because there was no time to wait for their dough to rise. Today, Jews all over the world observe Passover and eat matzos in memory of the hardships their ancestors suffered. Orthodox and Conservative Jews outside Israel observe the holiday for eight days, Reform Jews and Israeli Jews for seven.

Passover, like all Jewish holidays, begins at sundown. On the first and second nights of the holiday, Jewish families have a special feast called a *seder*. Before and after dinner, prayers are recited, songs are sung, and the story of the deliverance from Egypt is retold. Foods with symbolic significance—matzos, lamb, eggs, and wine—appear on the table and are part of the religious service.

The Passover story of delivery from bondage was to many Christians a foreshadowing of man's redemption from sin through the death and resurrection of Christ. Thus, in many ways the spring holidays of Easter and Passover remind us of the common heritage of Christians and Jews the world over.

EXERCISES

Comprehension. Choose the correct answer.

1. Easter owes its name and many of its customs to a pagan festival called
   (a) Eostre.
   (b) Passover.
   (c) Mardi Gras.

2. Easter celebrates
   (a) the harvest.
   (b) the Resurrection.
   (c) death.

3. The egg is a symbol of
   (a) the rising sun.
   (b) the Resurrection.
   (c) fertility.

4. The Easter bunny is a symbol of
   (a) the rising sun.
   (b) the Resurrection.
   (c) fertility.

5. The meats associated with Easter are
   (a) lamb and ham.
   (b) veal and mutton.
   (c) beef and chicken.

6. Lent honors the
   (a) Egyptian plagues.
   (b) tablets of Moses.
   (c) forty days Jesus spent in the desert.

7. Good Friday is the day of the
   (a) flight from Egypt.
   (b) Crucifixion.
   (c) Resurrection.

8. At the Last Supper, Jesus was celebrating
   (a) Yom Kippur.
   (b) Passover.
   (c) Yuan Tan.

9. While preparing to flee from Egypt, the Hebrews ate
   (a) Easter eggs.
   (b) ham
   (c) matzos.

10. Passover commemorates the
    (a) escape from Egypt.
    (b) Crucifixion.
    (c) New Year.

Vocabulary and Usage. Give the meaning of each of the following words. Use each in a sentence.

spring	awaken
rebirth	Resurrection
fertility	sacrifice
paradox	redemption
eternal	bondage

Conversation and Discussion. What similarities do you see between Passover and Easter? In what ways do they both symbolize rebirth?

XIV
Patriotic Holidays

In addition to the birthdays of Lincoln and Washington, Americans celebrate four other patriotic holidays: Memorial Day, Veterans Day, Flag Day, and Independence Day.

Memorial Day and Veterans Day are sad occasions; they recall the many lives that have been sacrificed to create and sustain the United States of America as an independent, unified, democratic nation. Flag Day and Independence Day are happy holidays which stimulate national pride in the courage and foresight of the colonists who first formed our country.

Memorial Day, originally established to honor the Civil War dead, now officially honors all American servicemen who gave their lives for their country. Unofficially, the holiday has been extended beyond its military connection to become a day of general tribute to the dead. On Memorial Day, cemeteries are crowded with families who come to place flowers on the graves of their loved ones.

Shortly after the bitter and bloody Civil War between the North and South, the women of Columbus, Mississippi decorated the graves of both Confederate and Union soldiers, thus honoring the war dead who were their enemies along with their defenders. Northerners were touched by this tender gesture and saw it as a symbol of national unity. In 1868, Decoration Day—now called Memorial Day—became a legal holiday.

In most states, Memorial Day is celebrated on the last Monday in May or on May 30. However, some Southern states observe Confederate Memorial Day in memory of the soldiers who fought in the Confederate army. This holiday falls on April 26 in Florida and Georgia, on the last Monday in April in Alabama and Mississippi, and on May 10 in North and South Carolina.

The military nature of Memorial Day is evident in the parades and customs which solemnly mark the occasion. Military exercises are held at Gettysburg National Military Park in Pennsylvania and at the National Cemetery in Arlington, Virginia.

Veterans Day, like Memorial Day, is a solemn occasion honoring America's servicemen. Originally, the holiday was called *Armistice Day*. It was established by President Wilson in 1919 to commemorate the signing of the armistice (on November 11, 1918) which brought an end to the fighting of World War I. In 1954, President Eisenhower signed a bill changing the name of the holiday to Veterans Day and extending its significance so that it now honors American veterans of all wars. It reminds us of the tragedies of war and is celebrated as "a day dedicated to world peace." Since the early 1970s, most states have been celebrating Veterans Day on the fourth Monday in October.

On Veterans Day, the flag is displayed and veterans march in parades in many communities. Special services are held at the tomb of the Unknown Soldier in Arlington National Cemetery. To Americans, the Unknown Soldier symbolizes all servicemen who have died in defense of their country.

Flag Day, June 14, is the birthday of the American flag. On this date in 1777, the Continental Congress adopted a resolution stating that the flag of the new nation should contain thirteen horizontal stripes (seven red ones and six white ones) to symbolize the thirteen colonies, and thirteen white stars arranged in a circle to symbolize the unity and equality of these colonies.

In 1776, after the colonies had declared their independence from Great Britain, George Washington and two other revolutionary leaders were assigned the task of designing a national flag. The colors they chose were red for courage, white for liberty, and blue for loyalty. According to American legend, they brought their design to Betsy

Ross, a young widow who was an excellent seamstress. She followed their sketch exactly, except for suggesting that the stars be five-pointed rather than six-pointed. Because she made the first American flag, Betsy Ross' name is still well-known to Americans. Her little home in Philadelphia has been preserved as a monument, and tens of thousands of tourists visit it each year.

The American flag has been redesigned many times since Betsy Ross made the original. Today, the flag still contains thirteen stripes in honor of the original colonies. But now there are fifty stars (one for each state) arranged in nine rows, alternating with six stars in one row and five in the next. Because of its design, the American flag has been nicknamed the "Stars and Stripes."

In school, children memorize and recite the following pledge of allegiance to the flag:

> I pledge allegiance to the flag of the United States of America and to the Republic for which it stands, one Nation under God, indivisible, with liberty and justice for all.

This pledge is recited with the right hand held over the heart to indicate love and devotion to the American flag and the nation it represents. Our national anthem, "The Star Spangled Banner," is also a tribute to the flag. It is sung at the opening of most public gatherings.

Independence Day, our most important patriotic holiday, celebrates the birth of the nation. In 1776, the thirteen American colonies were in the midst of their Revolutionary War against Great Britain. On the 4th of July of that year, the Continental Congress adopted the Declaration of Independence—a document which declared the colonies free and independent states. It is the signing and the significance of this document that Americans remember on July 4.

The Declaration of Independence was written by Thomas Jefferson, who later became the young nation's third President. Its most famous paragraph succinctly sums up the philosophical and political ideals of Americans from colonial days to the present:

> We hold these Truths to be self-evident, that all Men are created equal, that they are endowed by their Creator with certain unalienable Rights, that among these are Life, Liberty, and the Pursuit of Happiness—That to secure these Rights, Governments are instituted among Men, deriving their just Powers from the Consent of the Governed.

Since Independence Day is a summer holiday and a day off from work for almost everyone, many families enjoy picnics or beach outings on the Fourth. The occasion is also commemorated by colorful and noisy fireworks displays, parades, and, in some communities, patriotic speeches. The flag is flown and red, white, and blue ribbons are used for decoration at public ceremonies. The army marks the occasion by firing a thirteen-gun salute. Throughout the nation, church bells ring in memory of the Philadelphia Liberty Bell that first proclaimed American independence.

EXERCISES

Comprehension. Choose the correct answer.

1. Memorial Day was originally established to honor
   (a) the veterans of World War I.
   (b) the Civil War dead.
   (c) all American military dead.

2. Memorial Day now officially honors
   (a) the veterans of World War I.
   (b) the Civil War dead.
   (c) all American military dead.
3. On Memorial Day, people go to
   (a) homes.
   (b) churches.
   (c) cemeteries.
4. Veterans Day (once called Armistice Day) was originally established to celebrate
   (a) the end of World War I.
   (b) the creation of the American flag.
   (c) the signing of the Declaration of Independence.
5. Veterans Day now honors
   (a) the veterans of Viet Nam.
   (b) the American flag.
   (c) American veterans of all wars.
6. The Unknown Soldier symbolizes
   (a) the proclamation of American independence.
   (b) all American military dead.
   (c) the German armistice.
7. Flag Day is the
   (a) birth of the nation.
   (b) birthday of the American flag.
   (c) pledge of allegiance.
8. The first American flag was made by
   (a) George Washington.
   (b) Martha Washington.
   (c) Betsy Ross.
9. Independence Day celebrates
   (a) the signing of the Declaration of Independence.
   (b) the signing of the 1918 armistice.
   (c) the American military victory over the English.
10. The Declaration of Independence was written by
   (a) George Washington.
   (b) Abraham Lincoln.
   (c) Thomas Jefferson.

Vocabulary and Usage. Give the meaning of each of the following words. Use each in a sentence.

patriotic	armistice
independent	independence
military	defense
design	pledge
allegiance	consent

Conversation and Discussion. Name and describe some of the patriotic holidays of other countries.

XV
The American Cuisine

WHAT AND WHEN AMERICANS EAT

"Three square meals a day"—breakfast, lunch, and dinner—that's what the typical American is supposed to eat. However, if he adds between-meal snacks, as most Americans do, he probably eats five or six times a day.

Many American adults begin the day with just a small breakfast of juice or toast and coffee; but nutritionists recommend a heartier meal, and most parents therefore urge their children to eat more. In many households, breakfast is a sizable meal. The typical continental breakfast of a roll and coffee may be inadequate for Americans, who eat smaller lunches and earlier dinners than Europeans.

A complete American breakfast begins with fruit or fruit juice (usually orange juice). The main course generally consists of cereal or eggs. (The cereal can be either hot or cold. The eggs are accompanied by toast and perhaps bacon, ham, or sausages.) For adults, coffee is the usual breakfast drink. Other popular breakfast dishes are waffles, French toast (bread soaked in eggs and milk, then fried), and pancakes—all of which are served with butter and maple syrup.

The American who works the standard nine-to-five day usually eats breakfast around 8 A.M. By 10:30 or thereabouts, he is ready for the traditional mid-morning "coffee break." Most American workers are given ten to fifteen minutes off the job to have coffee and a doughnut or sweet roll.

Lunch hour is from noon until one o'clock or from one until two. People at work or school rarely go home for lunch. Instead, many bring lunch with them from home. For this purpose they need a meal that is small, portable, and does not require constant refrigeration. The sandwich meets all three requirements. In addition, it is inexpensive and easy to prepare. The sandwich chef needs only two pieces of bread (or three for a club sandwich), something moist to smear on the bread (butter, mayonnaise, mustard, or catsup), and some meat, cheese, fish, or poultry slices to stuff in between. Some popular cold sandwiches are those made with ham and cheese, peanut butter and jelly, sliced chicken or turkey, tuna salad, or roast beef. Lettuce, tomato, and pickle are often tucked inside or served alongside the sandwich.

People who eat lunch in restaurants are more likely to order hot sandwiches. The most popular of these are hamburgers and hot dogs. Hamburgers are patties of chopped meat, usually served in round buns. Hot dogs are five-inch red sausages (sometimes called red hots, frankfurters, or wieners) served in long buns. Toasted cheese sandwiches and cheeseburgers (hamburgers topped with melted cheese) are also popular.

For a bigger lunch, one might add a bowl of soup before the sandwich, French fried potatoes or potato chips with it, and a sweet dessert or fruit afterwards. With lunch, children usually drink milk or a carbonated beverage. Adults prefer coffee, tea, or perhaps beer.

Because most people eat lunch around the same time, restaurants are quite crowded between noon and two o'clock. At counters, where customers sit on a row of stools rather than at separate tables, waitresses can provide faster service. To save time, many people eat in cafeterias, where customers walk by displays of food, place what they want on their trays, then pay a cashier at the end of the line. Self-service cafeterias handle big crowds quickly and efficiently. In large institutions such as factories, hospitals, and schools, there are usually cafeterias or lunchrooms with food-dispensing machines from which customers can purchase soup, sandwiches, drinks, fruit, and sweets. Equipment for heating foods is usually set up near these machines.

The mid-afternoon snack, like the mid-morning snack, may be just a drink or may include cake, candy, or ice cream. After school, children particularly like an ice-cream snack. For a dime or fifteen cents, a youngster can buy an ice-cream cone or bar. For twenty-five to fifty cents, he can buy an ice-cream soda, milk shake, malted, or sundae. Ice-cream sodas contain two scoops of ice cream in flavored, carbonated water. Milk shakes and malteds are thick, whipped drinks made with ice cream, milk, and the customer's choice of flavoring. Sundaes are dishes of ice cream topped with flavoring and sometimes fruit or cookies. The most impressive and expensive sundae is the banana split, with several scoops of ice cream, banana slices, chocolate sauce, nuts, and whipped cream.

In the U.S.A., the biggest meal of the day is dinner, served about six o'clock. Usually, children older than five eat with their parents, whereas younger children may be fed earlier. Dinner includes several courses: an appetizer (fresh fruit, fruit juice, or a small portion of fish), soup, salad, an entree (meat, poultry, or fish served with a cooked vegetable and potatoes, rice, or noodles), coffee (or tea), and dessert. The European custom of ending the meal with fruit and cheese is not very popular in this country. Most Americans prefer a sweet dessert: cake, pie, cookies, ice cream, or sherbet. "As American as apple pie," people often say. And it is true that apple pie, often served hot with a scoop of ice cream (à la mode) or a slice of cheese, is a favorite throughout the nation.

With lunch and dinner, Americans commonly drink water, a fruit juice, coffee, tea, or soda (a carbonated drink that may be cola-flavored or contain an imitation fruit flavor). Though children are urged to drink milk with every meal, many prefer soda or juice instead. Among adults, beer is quite popular, especially with men. Though many Americans customarily serve wine with dinner, the majority do not. However, wine is considered festive and is likely to appear on holidays, at celebrations, and when dining out. Stronger alcoholic beverages (cocktails) and hors d'oeuvres are frequently served before dinner, particularly at parties.

Since dinner is customarily served early in the evening,

the late evening snack is a ritual in most households. Children often have milk and cookies before bedtime. Adults may nibble on fruit or sweets.

On weekends and holidays, the meal schedule may vary. In many families, Sunday *brunch* is traditional. Brunch, as its name implies, is a combination of breakfast and lunch. It is served between eleven o'clock and noon and usually includes typical breakfast foods plus cheese, fruit, cake, and perhaps cold fish. Brunch should be substantial enough to sustain one until dinner time.

Families who go to church on Sunday morning may have their usual weekday breakfast before services and then eat their biggest meal of the day about two o'clock. The main meal is always called *dinner*, no matter what time it is served. When dinner is eaten in mid-afternoon, a smaller evening meal, called *supper*, is served around seven o'clock. On Saturday evenings, many people eat very late dinners, particularly those who dine out. Crowds begin to pour into restaurants about seven o'clock, and some people dine continental style as late as nine or ten o'clock.

On Sundays and holidays when the weather is mild, American families often eat outdoors. Picnics in parks, backyard barbecues (usually featuring charcoal-broiled steaks or hamburgers), Fourth of July neighborhood wiener roasts, and clambakes (New England-style picnics where clams, lobsters, potatoes, and corn are steamed on a bed of hot stones under a layer of wet seaweed) are all popular.

Sunday is traditionally a day of rest, and many American women also take a rest from the kitchen. Families often go out for a casual Sunday dinner. Those with young children may enjoy a quick and inexpensive meal at a drive-in restaurant, where food is brought to and eaten in the car.

When Mom doesn't want to cook, another possibility is to "order out." Dad may phone a carry-out restaurant, order the family's dinner, then either drive over to pick it up or ask to have it delivered. Ordering out is one way to introduce children to foreign styles of cooking, since many carry-out restaurants specialize in Chinese or Italian cuisine.

In the U.S.A., as elsewhere, eating is an important part of family life and social activity. In many homes, dinner time may be the only time when everyone gets together and shares the day's experiences. Families get to know one another and make joint decisions around the dinner table. Dinner time is also an occasion for inviting friends. Americans frequently entertain at home, both formally and informally.

Dining out is also an important part of American social life. For single men and women, dates often begin with dinner in a nice restaurant. Married couples often get together in groups to eat out, especially on weekends. In their desire to use time efficiently, Americans may rush through breakfast and gulp down lunch. But dinner is usually a more leisurely meal at which enjoyment of good food is enhanced by the presence of pleasant company.

EXERCISES

Comprehension. Choose the correct answer.

1. Americans commonly begin the day by drinking
   (a) soda.
   (b) cocktails.
   (c) orange juice.

2. In mid-morning, most Americans have
   (a) a glass of wine.
   (b) some eggs.
   (c) coffee.
3. For lunch, many Americans eat
   (a) a sandwich.
   (b) beer and sausage.
   (c) brunch.
4. The mid-morning snack is called
   (a) tea-time.
   (b) a coffee break.
   (c) a work break.
5. A meal that combines breakfast and lunch is called
   (a) supper.
   (b) brunch.
   (c) dinner.
6. For dessert, most Americans prefer
   (a) something sweet.
   (b) nothing.
   (c) fruit and cheese.
7. The main meal of the day is always called
   (a) supper.
   (b) a snack.
   (c) dinner.
8. Sunday is a
   (a) day of rest.
   (b) regular working day.
   (c) school day.
9. Meals eaten outdoors are called
   (a) restaurants.
   (b) picnics.
   (c) snacks.
10. Americans eat about
   (a) five times a day.
   (b) twice a day.
   (c) three times a day.

Vocabulary and Usage. Give the meaning of each of the following words. Use each in a sentence.

substantial	favorite
beverage	cafeteria
service	prefer
self-service	display
enhance	efficiency

Conversation and Discussion. Compare the eating habits of Americans with those found in other countries.

XVI
Evaluating the American Diet

Nowhere are American prosperity and ingenuity more apparent than in the kitchen and on the dinner table. In the U.S.A., food is abundant, tasty, inexpensive, and easy to prepare. More than enough food to feed 212 million people is produced by less than 5 percent of the population. (In India, food production occupies 90 percent of the people; in Russia, 45 percent.) In many poorer countries, foods from plants—especially grains such as wheat or rice—constitute 70 to 85 percent of the people's diet. But in the United States, as in most European countries, meat, fish, poultry, and dairy products constitute about 40 percent of the typical diet.

The American diet is probably more varied than that of any other country, due, in part, to its international flavor. Housewives often prepare continental entrees such as veal parmesan, chicken cacciatore, beef burgundy, and duckling with orange sauce. In the supermarkets, there are frozen blintzes, Chinese egg roll, pizza, and dozens of other foreign dishes all ready to be warmed and eaten. Spaghetti, cooked or uncooked and with or without Italian sauce, can be purchased in almost every grocery store. Shops that specialize in imported canned goods may carry such exotic items as hearts of palm from Brazil, jellied pickled eels from Sweden, and kangaroo tail soup from Australia.

Regional food specialties add further variety to the American diet. From New England come wonderful seafood chowders (usually clams or lobsters stewed with vegetables and milk), baked beans, brown breads, and Boston cream pie. Southerners have created delicious recipes for fried chicken, smoked ham, grits (a side dish made with corn meal, milk, and eggs), and fritters (small, fried cakes often containing fruit). New Orleans is famous for its Creole cooking, which combines French, Spanish, Negro, and American Indian culinary arts. Especially popular nationwide are the shrimp and chicken Creole dishes, which have exotic, spicy sauces. The western part of the country has adopted many specialties created by its residents of Chinese and Mexican descent. Among the Mexican foods, tamales, enchiladas, tacos, and chili con carne are well-known throughout the United States.

Because of a diversified climate and geography, a great variety of fruits and vegetables can be grown in the United States. These can be quickly transported in refrigerated railroad cars and sold hundreds or even thousands of miles from where they were produced. Throughout the nation, Americans enjoy fresh tomatoes from Texas, oranges from Florida, and strawberries from California. High-quality fruits, juices, and vegetables are available any time of the year, thanks to modern freezing techniques.

A substantial number of Americans are not only well-fed; they are also overfed. Many Americans overeat in relation to the amount of physical exercise they get. Automobiles, elevators, escalators, power lawn mowers, and a multitude of other mechanical devices rob Americans of the exercise they need to burn up food energy. Experts say that one-third of Americans are overweight and one-fifth have a serious weight problem.

"Everything enjoyable in life is either illegal, immoral, or fattening," moan those who are overweight. To help take the deprivation out of dieting, the American food industry has produced a wide assortment of dietetic foods. These are made without sugar, using artificial sweeteners which have no food value. In most supermarkets, dieters can find low-calorie beverages, ice cream, cookies, jelly, syrup, and canned fruit. There are also nutritious canned drinks and complete frozen meals for people who want to take off excess weight. Why all this emphasis upon staying thin? It is partly because doctors say that extra weight decreases life expectancy. It is also vanity; a slim figure is basic to the American ideal of feminine beauty, and a "potbelly" detracts from a man's appearance, too.

Helping people take off pounds has become big business in the United States. In addition to dietetic foods, the public is offered special slenderizing clothes, exercise equipment for the home, weight reduction parlors stressing steam and exercise, and residential camps (some for adults, some for children). In recent years, an American-born organization called Weight Watchers has become a phenomenal success. The Weight Watchers program includes a high-protein diet plus weekly meetings at which members receive tips on dieting, insights into why they overeat, and moral support and encouragement from each other. Between 1965 and 1973, about 3 million people attended Weight Watchers meetings. Weight Watchers franchises operate in forty-nine states and some foreign countries and take in about $45 million annually. The parent company is a multi-million dollar business with stock on the open market. The company puts out a cookbook, a magazine, and a line of low-calorie frozen foods. Other clubs for dieters also use the weekly meeting and the "buddy system" (a fellow member to phone for support when the chocolate cake seems irresistible).

The organized camaraderie among dieters is similar to the approach of Alcoholics Anonymous, a fellowship of men and women who share their experiences and help each other solve their common drinking problem. Alcoholics Anonymous has about 400,000 members in 14,000 local groups in the United States and abroad. It is unfortunate that the organization is not much larger because in the United States there are about nine million alcoholics.

Those who are not counting calories or cocktails may be concerned about cholesterol count. The American diet includes much fatty meat, butter, ice cream, fried foods, and other sources of saturated fats (those that are solid at room temperature). Solid fats are high in cholesterol, and medical researchers have discovered that people with high cholesterol levels are likely to develop some kinds of circulatory disorders. Thus, many Americans are under doctors' orders to cut down on the intake of cholesterol. The typical American diet is a serious threat to the health of middle-aged men and older people.

Another possible threat to the health of Americans comes from chemicals added to foods. These can be divided into three major categories: pesticides and herbicides used in growing plants; additives used in some packaged foods; and drugs fed to beef cattle.

For the sake of efficiency and economy, American farmers use large quantities of chemical pesticides. These increase crop yield and protect crops from destruction by insects and other animals, thus keeping the supply of fruits and vegetables up and prices down. However, the scientific community and many citizens are worried about the effect that these chemicals may have upon animals (including the human animal) that consume them. Rachel Carson's alarming book, *Silent Spring*, describes (among other horrors) a world without the songs of birds. Since her book appeared in 1962, many people have asked such questions as: "To what degree will the poison sprayed on foods to kill rats injure human beings?" No one seems to know the answer.

Similar concerns involve chemicals, such as coloring, flavoring, or preservatives, added to packaged foods. Many of the products that are now frowned upon have been used for decades. Until recently, most packaged bread sold in the United States contained a preservative. Many pre-cooked foods and seasoning mixes contain a flavor enhancer that may be harmful in large quantities. One of the popular artificial sweeteners was taken off the market a few years ago. Most nutritionists disapprove of the chemical used to preserve and color luncheon meats. As a result of recent public concern and scientific research, several chemicals which once were commonly added to foods at the rate of thousands of tons a year are now banned, and many more are undergoing rigorous investigation.

Then there is the matter of giving drugs to beef cattle. Until the government banned its use, a cancer-producing hormone was routinely given to livestock to help fatten them up. But antibiotics continue to be administered in order to prevent the spread of infection among animals crowded together in close quarters. The long-range effect of these drugs upon the meat-eating public is unknown.

Some people are so worried about the dangers of all these chemicals that they go to much trouble and expense to obtain "organic" foods produced without chemicals. One way to be sure that your fruits and vegetables are not sprayed is to grow your own, and many people do. Others shop at special farms or stores that sell (or claim to sell) only organically grown products. Some people travel long distances to purchase meat at ranches where animals are not given any drugs. The general public labels these people "health nuts," and most food producers agree. They say that the effect of chemical additives is insignificant, and discontinuing their use would mean smaller harvests, less prime beef, faster spoilage, and generally higher food prices.

This debate has made the American public pay more attention than ever to the ingredients in the foods they eat. The government insists that all ingredients be listed on packaged foods, and housewives are now reading those labels carefully. Pressure for stricter government control of the food industry has been growing as more and more Americans demand that consumers get a fair deal.

Putting aside the possible dangers of chemical additives, it would seem that Americans should be well-nourished. Every kind of food necessary for life is available here, and most Americans have sufficient income to afford a well-balanced diet. Yet, malnutrition and undernourishment are not rare in this wealthiest of nations. Among some of the poorer minority groups, malnutrition is commonplace. Among teen-agers and older people, undernourishment frequently occurs. Many teen-agers often eat "junk" foods with little nutritional value. Instead of milk and fruit juices, they drink beverages that are essentially water, sugar, and artificial flavoring. According to a recent study, Americans over sixty show evidence of gradual undernutrition, and this is not restricted to the poor. Many elderly people living alone don't care enough or are not well enough to prepare well-balanced meals for themselves. And some cannot afford to do so.

On the positive side, evidence shows that the general health and nutrition of Americans has improved markedly during the twentieth century. Soldiers in World War II were found to be much healthier than those of World War I, and the credit was given primarily to better diet. The once prevalent deficiency diseases (rickets, pellagra, and scurvy) have practically disappeared in the United States. This improvement is partly because of the nation's generally higher standard of living and partly because many of our basic foods (including milk and many grain products) are required by state laws to be fortified with additional vitamins and minerals.

Although Americans in all income brackets complain about the high cost of food (particularly meat), comparisons show that in this country food is a bargain. Prices here may seem high in relation to those in other countries, but when considered in terms of the average American's income, they are quite low. For example, the average New Yorker works about six minutes to earn the price of a quart of milk; in Moscow, twenty-four minutes of work is required. Americans spend 16 percent of their disposable income for food. In every other industrial nation, food takes a much bigger percentage of the disposable income. In Germany, the figure is 22 percent; in Italy, nearly 32 percent; in Japan, 33 percent. However, these figures do not represent typical middle income expenditures. In the United States, the family with an annual income of $100,000 may spend less than 5 percent of its income on food, while the family earning $10,000 a year may spend 30 percent of it on groceries. In general, a moderate income family of four (earning between $10,000 and $15,000 a year) spends between $35 and $60 per week on food, 20 to 25 percent of the family's disposable income.

While the family breadwinner should be grateful for his low food bills, the American housewife should also count her blessings. Innovations in food processing, packaging, and marketing, as well as technological advancements in kitchen gadgetry, have freed her from hours of daily drudgery preparing meals. Today she can shop, cook, and clean up the kitchen with amazing speed and efficiency.

In the not-too-distant past, to buy food for the family's dinner, the American housewife had to trudge from bakery to butcher shop to grocery store to fish store. Today, she can find everything she needs in food, cleaning items, and even basic cooking utensils in one store—the supermarket. Most supermarkets are part of national chains with hundreds, sometimes thousands, of branches throughout the nation, totaling billions of dollars in annual sales. These chains are owned by thousands of stockholders who share in their profits.

In the supermarket, the housewife uses a metal cart to carry her purchases. She pushes her cart up and down aisle after aisle of canned, packaged, and frozen foods, selecting what she wants. She can stop to read labels and compare prices, and after selecting certain brands and sizes, she can change her mind and put a package back on the shelf.

When she is through shopping, she wheels her cart to the cashier, who totals her bill and takes her money. Frequently, supermarket chains, which are competing for customers, offer bonus stamps (these can be exchanged for free merchandise) or run contests.

For the shopper without a car, many supermarkets offer delivery service. This service costs about fifty cents or more, depending upon the amount of merchandise purchased. Some housewives fill their carts to the brim so that they need shop only once or twice a week. Storing enough food for a week of meals is no problem for the woman who has a separate home freezer or a refrigerator with a large freezing compartment.

In modern America, not only shopping is quicker and easier than ever before; cooking is, too. Many of the foods that the American housewife buys are partly or wholly prepared for her. A great variety of soups and sauces come in cans or in small packages. The housewife just adds water, heats, and serves. Other timesavers include mixes for making mashed potatoes, pancakes, cookies, and cakes. To these, the housewife adds just two or three ingredients—usually butter, milk, and eggs. There are also instant beverages—coffee, cocoa, lemonade, and many others—to which she adds only water. Most frozen foods are precooked and need only to be heated.

The ultimate in cooking ease is the TV dinner, a three- or four-course frozen meal packaged in an aluminum tray. The housewife merely puts the tray into the oven for about a half-hour, serves the meal right in its tray, then discards the container. No pots or dishes to wash; no lost time. Portions are small, but prices are low. For emergency meals when the woman of the house comes home late or must rush away for the evening, TV dinners are extremely handy. They come in foreign cooking styles, such as Mexican, Italian, and Chinese; but typical American dinners, such as meat loaf or sliced turkey, are also available.

Prepared foods, convenient though they are, have not replaced home cooking. The American woman is taught that "the way to a man's heart is through his stomach." She can and does cook her own dinners but doesn't have to stay home all day to do it. If she has an automatic oven, she can set the dial to turn the heat on and off automatically. Her chicken or chocolate cake can be baking while she goes to the hairdresser or walks the baby. After dinner, she can put the dirty dishes in the electric dishwasher and watch television with her family. The modern American woman can spend less time being a housekeeper and more time being a wife and mother thanks to the inventiveness of the American food and electronics industries.

EXERCISES

Comprehension. Choose the correct answer.

1. The American diet is most notable for its
   (a) monotony.
   (b) variety.
   (c) expense.

2. A city which is famous for its Creole food is
   (a) New York.
   (b) San Francisco.
   (c) New Orleans.

3. Fresh fruits and vegetables are often transported great distances in
   (a) carts.
   (b) elevators.
   (c) refrigerated railroad cars.
4. In the United States there is no problem of
   (a) alcoholism.
   (b) malnutrition.
   (c) famine.
5. The proportion of Americans who are overweight is about
   (a) one out of three.
   (b) one out of seven.
   (c) one out of nine.
6. The percentage of his income that an American spends on food is
   (a) low
   (b) medium.
   (c) high.
7. A store where the housewife can buy almost everything in one stop is called a
   (a) supermarket.
   (b) market.
   (c) grocery.
8. Most supermarkets are part of
   (a) grocery stores.
   (b) bakeries.
   (c) national chains.
9. The time that the American housewife spends preparing meals has
   (a) increased.
   (b) decreased.
   (c) remained the same.
10. Many frozen foods are
    (a) cereals.
    (b) precooked.
    (c) mixes.

Vocabulary and Usage. Give the meaning of each of the following words. Use each in a sentence.

flavor	specialty
seasoning	diversified
abundant	variety
nutrition	slim
trudge	diet

Conversation and Discussion. What is your favorite food? How is it prepared?

XVII
American Education

THE ACADEMIC LEVELS

Education is "like a big window opening," according to the English novelist Mary Webb. Americans are proud of the fact that the window of knowledge is never slammed shut for any of the nation's citizens. All American children are offered twelve years of free public education, and most good students can get financial help to continue their studies for many more years. Adults who wish to attend school also find many opportunities. In this nation of rapid change, there can be no age limit on learning; everyone must study—in classrooms or independently—to keep in touch with the changing life around him.

Early Childhood Education

In most areas, free public school education begins with kindergarten classes for five-year-olds. Through these half-day sessions (usually two to three hours long), the child becomes accustomed to being separated from Mommy, playing and sharing with other children, and following the directions of a teacher. He is also introduced to skills and information that will help him later with academic work. For example, he learns the colors and the alphabet, how to write his name, to count to ten, to work with art supplies, and to enjoy books. Early childhood education is considered so beneficial that some public school systems also offer pre-kindergarten programs for four-year-olds, though some tuition is usually charged.

Nearly three million American children attend kindergarten each year. For many, kindergarten is their first school experience. But some are introduced to the classroom situation at a much younger age, either through nursery schools or day care centers.

Nursery schools accept children from three to five years old for half-day sessions ranging from twice a week to five days a week. The typical nursery school classroom is equipped much like a kindergarten, with dolls, toy furniture, building blocks, books, puzzles, and art supplies. Most nursery schools (like schools for older children) have an outdoor playground. A youngster who has no playmates his age living nearby may benefit greatly from attending nursery school. Nursery schools usually charge tuition, though some are subsidized and some offer scholarships.

Day care centers provide care for pre-school children of working mothers who need a place to leave their children all day, five days a week. Some day care centers accept pre-schoolers from infancy on. The children have lunch and snacks at the center and spend the entire day there. Day care has been maligned by those who believe that children belong with their mothers and that "a woman's place is in the home." But more and more women are coming to believe that motherhood should not be their sole occupation. The Women's Liberation movement, which became extremely prominent in the 1960s, has widely publicized the idea that free, high-quality day care is essential if women are to participate fully in society.

At the present time, the need for more day care centers is acute. For the six million pre-school children whose mothers are working, there are only 625,000 openings in certified day care centers. Many working mothers pay a large percentage of their earnings to babysitters; many take turns with other mothers to provide day care for small groups of children in their homes; some, in desperation, leave their pre-schoolers alone all day.

Existing day care centers are operated and funded by many different organizations. Some are profit-making facilities supported by tuition fees. Others are non-profit centers run by philanthropic, religious, governmental, or industrial sponsors. These are subsidized by the sponsoring agency and charge a graduated fee according to income. Organizations that employ a large number of women (hospitals, federal agencies, and several large corporations) have become involved in the establishment of day care centers, as have many universities and a few unions. Also, some communities have pre- and post-school programs for school-age children whose mothers leave for work before school begins and come home after school lets out.

About 30 percent of mothers with children under age six are now in the labor force. Government statistics predict that between 1975 and 1985 there will be a 32 percent increase in the number of working mothers with pre-school children. So, although the federal government is already spending more than a billion dollars a year on day care, there will certainly be continued pressure for increased public support.

Grammar School and High School

In the United States, classes of students are divided into twelve academic levels called *grades*. Generally, one academic year (from September through June) is required to complete each grade. Academic work—learning to read, write, and do arithmetic—begins when the child enters first grade, at about age six.

The first academic institution that a child attends is called *grammar school* or *elementary school*. In some school systems, elementary school includes grades one through eight. The next four years are called *high school*. In other school systems, there are three divisions: *elementary school* (grades one through six), *junior high school* (grades seven through nine), and *senior high school* (grades ten through twelve).

The typical elementary school day starts at 9:00 A.M. and ends about 3:30 P.M. Junior high and high school students usually attend classes from 8:30 A.M. until 3:30 P.M. For all levels, schools are in session five days a week, Monday through Friday. Traditional vacation periods of one to two weeks are scheduled at Christmas and in the spring, and the schools also close for certain holidays. Most students do not go to school during July or August, unless they enroll in summer sessions.

Grammar schools teach reading, arithmetic, and language arts such as creative writing, spelling, and handwriting. Social studies, science, music, art, and physical education (athletics) are also part of the program. In high school, subject matter becomes more specialized. English classes stress grammar and literature. Social studies is split into separate courses in American history, American government, and European history. Algebra, geometry, and trigonometry are offered. High school students usually take a one-year general science course, then more detailed courses in biology, chemistry, and physics. Most high school students study a foreign language—usually Latin, French, Spanish, or German. Courses in music, art, and physical education are often required. Some high schools specialize in vocational education and train students for various technical careers.

During the elementary years, students are grouped into classes, and each group stays together for the entire school day and the entire school year. Generally, the class has the same teacher for most subjects, although art, music, and physical education are usually taught by teachers who specialize in these areas. In most high schools, students meet with a different teacher and a different group of students for each subject. The high school student's day may be divided into nine periods: five for academic subjects, one session for physical education, a lunch period, and two study periods. The study periods may be used for visiting the library or participating in an extracurricular activity such as the school orchestra, newspaper staff, or math club.

Colleges and Universities

When a student graduates from high school, he may attend college if his high school record and test scores are good enough to gain him admittance. American education on the college level (sometimes called *higher education*) is provided by more than 3,000 institutions. They range in size from very small schools serving only a few hundred students to huge state universities with student bodies exceeding 40,000. Some are supported privately and some by local and/or state governments. Some admit only men and some only women, but most are coeducational. Some are called colleges, which means that they offer only undergraduate courses. Others are called universities, which means that they have undergraduate, graduate, and professional schools. Recently, more and more junior colleges (offering the first two years of college only) have been established.

Since World War II, one of the most dramatic developments in higher education has been the enormous increase in the number of students. In 1939, about 1.5 million men and women were enrolled in the nation's colleges and universities. By 1970, the number had grown to 8.5 million; estimates for 1980 run to 11 million. To meet this demand, colleges and universities have expanded tremendously. Between 1945 and 1967, 300 university branches were established. In addition, many new schools have been built. This huge expansion reflects the nation's population explosion as well as a trend toward democratizing higher education. Today, a college education is seen as the right of any capable student rather than as a privilege reserved for the wealthy.

Colleges and universities offer a vast array of subjects. The student can sample different fields of knowledge, but he usually concentrates (majors) in one field during his last two years of college. If he wishes, he may obtain professional training at the undergraduate level, for example, in accounting, teaching, journalism, or dramatics. Certain state colleges specialize in training agricultural experts and engineers. For those who wish to prepare for military careers, the United States government maintains four special academies.

At the college level, the academic year is about nine months long (usually from mid-September until early June or from late August until May). After completing four academic years with acceptable grades in an approved course of study, the student earns a bachelor's degree. Some students complete college in less than four years by attending summer sessions. At most colleges, the academic year is divided into either two or three semesters, excluding the summer session. College grades, from highest to lowest, run *A, B, C, D, F*. An *F* is a failing grade; if a student receives an *F* in a particular course, he does not get credit for having taken the course. College students must maintain at least a low *C* average in order to remain in school.

American universities offer three main categories of graduate degrees. In most fields of specialization, a master's degree can be earned by one or two academic years of study beyond the bachelor's degree. A Ph.D. degree (doctor of philosophy) usually takes at least three years beyond the master's. To earn a Ph.D. in almost any field, the student must generally pass oral and written examinations in his specialty, produce a long research paper which makes an original contribution to his field of study, and pass reading examinations in one or two foreign languages. There are also graduate professional schools in medicine, dentistry, and law, among other fields.

A college community is an interesting and lively place. Students become involved in many different activities —extracurricular, religious, social, and athletic. Among the extracurricular activities are college newspapers, musical organizations, dramatic clubs, and political groups. Some of these have faculty advisers. Many religious groups have their own meeting places where services and social activities can be held. Student groups run parties of all types—from formal dances to picnics. Most colleges have a *student union* where students can get together for lunch, study sessions, club meetings, and socializing.

At many schools, campus life revolves around fraternities (social and, in some cases, residential clubs for men) and sororities (similar clubs for women). These organizations exist on more than 500 campuses. The best known are national groups with many *chapters* at schools throughout the country. Their names are Greek letters such as Alpha Delta Phi. These groups have been much criticized for being cruel and prejudiced because membership is limited and selective. A student must be invited to join. There is often great competition among freshmen and sophomores who want to join. Those who seek membership must go through *rush* (a period when prospective members visit different *houses* to meet and be evaluated by current members). The whole experience can be very painful if a student goes through *rush* and then is not asked to *pledge* (become a trial member of) any of the houses he or she has visited. Sororities and fraternities also tend to limit membership to one particular racial and religious group, thereby depriving its members of the wonderful opportunity that college offers for broadening social contacts. However, these groups do help students find friends of similar backgrounds; thus, they help combat loneliness for those away from home.

Athletics is an important phase of life on most campuses. In addition to required physical education courses, voluntary programs are provided for health, recreation, and the development of teams for intercollegiate competition. Most coeducational and men's schools belong to an athletic league. The teams within the league play against each other, aiming for the league championship. Football is the college sport which stirs up the most national interest. At large schools, promoting football, developing a team, and playing before huge crowds have become a big business. Season tickets are sold for substantial prices. Games, complete with student marching bands and entertainment, are major productions. Other sports —particularly basketball, swimming, and track—are also pursued with enthusiasm. Some schools have competitive tennis, skiing, sailing, wrestling, soccer, and baseball.

College campuses are attracting students from all social classes despite the rapidly rising cost of higher education. The cost of a college education has doubled within the last fifteen years and tripled within the last thirty. A typical college now charges about $3,000 a year for room, board, and tuition. The student attending a private Eastern college spends at least $3,500 and probably closer to $5,000 a year, including tuition, housing, food, books, and personal expenses. At the other end of the scale, a student attending a state college in a rural area may get by on $1,500 a year. State colleges and universities have rather low tuition fees (ranging from about $60 to about $450) for state residents. In some communities, low-cost public education is available at city colleges or junior colleges.

Fortunately for students with limited funds, financial help is available from many sources. Every year college students receive more than $300 million in monetary assistance, including scholarships, loans, and part-time jobs. More than 200,000 scholarships are offered by industries, alumni groups, individual donors, the federal government, and colleges and universities. The "G.I. Bill," passed in 1944, was the first in a series of laws giving financial help to armed forces veterans. A student may cut costs by living at home, attending a state or community school, or combining part-time work with a part-time college program. Many college students use their summer earnings to help finance their education. Some students pursue undergraduate or graduate degrees in night school while working full time during the day. Some college courses are offered on television, and these are inexpensive.

Many young people from poor families struggle along on limited budgets in order to stay in school because they know that a college degree brings higher income, greater job security, more prestige, and a more significant career. "Every son must rise above his father" is a major aspect of the American Dream—and one that is most often realized through higher education.

EXERCISES

Comprehension. Choose the correct answer.

1. The first academic training that an American child receives is in
   (a) high school.
   (b) parochial school.
   (c) grammar school.

2. In the American school system, there are twelve levels called
   (a) grades.
   (b) high school.
   (c) kindergarten.

3. The combined elementary and high school levels of education last for
   (a) ten years.
   (b) twelve years.
   (c) fourteen years.
4. In high school, subject matter becomes more
   (a) general.
   (b) specialized.
   (c) interesting.
5. In 1970, American institutions of higher learning enrolled about
   (a) two million students.
   (b) three million students.
   (c) eight million students.
6. The expansion of educational institutions reflects, in part, the
   (a) population explosion.
   (b) array of subjects.
   (c) increasing costs.
7. The highest degree which an American university awards is the
   (a) B.S.
   (b) Ph.D.
   (c) M.A.
8. The major obstacle to democratic educational opportunities is
   (a) junior college.
   (b) scholarships.
   (c) cost.
9. The average yearly cost of education at private universities is about
   (a) $1,000
   (b) $10,000.
   (c) $4,000.

10. The "G.I. Bill" provides financial help to
    (a) veterans.
    (b) black students.
    (c) foreign students.

Vocabulary and Usage. Give the meaning of each of the following words. Use each in a sentence.

graduate	enormous
expansion	capable
tuition	category
maligned	involve
scholarship	require

Conversation and Discussion. Imagine that you are a student in an American university. What kinds of courses would you like to study? What activities would you want to join?

American Education

PHILOSOPHY, METHODS, AND GOALS

XVIII
American Education

PHILOSOPHY, METHODS, PROBLEMS, GOALS

Education in the United States has been shaped by the American belief in a free, democratic society. In turn, education has helped to shape that society. The survival of a democracy depends upon the intelligent participation of all its citizens. Every American needs to be educated so that he can understand and take part in affairs of government, both local and national. He must also have educational opportunities to develop vocational skills. Education is the key that opens the doors to responsible citizenship and a productive life.

Americans believe that every citizen has both the right and the obligation to become educated. This philosophy accounts for the nation's extremely low illiteracy rate (about one percent). All states have compulsory school attendance laws. Children must go to school until they are at least sixteen years old, unless they are severely handicapped. But most Americans go to school well past the age of sixteen. About 80 percent of American teen-agers complete high school. Almost 50 percent of today's high school graduates enroll in institutions of higher learning. American colleges and universities graduate about one million students a year.

The size of the American educational enterprise is astonishing. About 60 million people, approximately 28 percent of the nation's total population, are enrolled in grammar schools, high schools, colleges, and universities. Another 9 million attend trade schools, and 13 million participate in adult education through schools, job training, correspondence courses, community organizations, or tutors. Many high schools, colleges, and community centers offer noncredit daytime or evening classes in dozens of skills such as speed-reading, sewing, cooking, child care, judo, and photography. Courses in English as a foreign language and in American government (to prepare immigrants for the citizenship exam) are also commonly available.

To educate this vast number of students, American schools employ about 2.5 million teachers. Teachers are by far the largest professional group in the country.

In the United States, some schools are public and others are private. The names *public* and *private* refer to the manner in which the schools are supported and controlled. Public schools are tax-supported and controlled by local officials. Private schools generally charge tuition and are not under direct public control, although many states set educational standards for private schools. Private schools can be divided into two categories: parochial (those supported by various religious groups) and nondenominational. Parochial schools make up the largest segment of private schools, and most of these are operated by the Roman Catholic Church. Private nondenominational schools are mainly high schools and colleges. Public schools, which educate about 88 percent of American children, have brought the American ideals of universal education and equal opportunity for all closest to realization.

American public schools have four basic characteristics in common: they are locally controlled, free from religious influence, coeducational, and publicly supported by taxes. Each state elects or appoints a state Board of Education which establishes general policies. For example, the Board sets teacher qualification standards for its own schools. But the states entrust the actual operation of schools to local school districts. Keeping operational control local brings the school and the community closer together and enables the school to do a better job of meeting the needs of the community.

Separation of church and state is a basic guarantee of the United States Constitution. As applied to education, this means that no religious doctrine can be taught in public schools. Because American public schools are nonsectarian, children from all types of religious backgrounds can attend classes together. Nonsectarian public education has helped a diverse population build a common culture.

Coeducational public schools have enabled girls to prove that they possess as much intellectual potential as boys. The self-sufficiency of the American woman can be attributed, in large part, to her unlimited educational opportunities.

Taxes paid by all adults, whether they have children attending or not, support the public schools. Taxes collected by local districts and states make up about 93 percent of the revenue. The small balance comes from the federal government. The state levies taxes in a variety of ways and spends a percentage of its income on the schools. Generally, the state distributes funds for education to state colleges, universities, and local school districts. In addition, local school districts raise money from property taxes. Local districts spend their funds primarily on elementary and high schools. School districts vary greatly in their ability to assess taxes. Wealthy districts have much more money to spend on their schools than poor districts. The states, attempting to realize the ideal of equal educational opportunity for all, have tried to develop ways of giving more state tax money to the poor districts. This policy has met with some success, but there is still inequality in school systems throughout the land.

Americans now spend about $86 billion annually on education. What does the nation expect to gain from this huge investment? Ideas of what schools should teach and how schools should teach have been altered greatly since earlier times. In the nineteenth century, high schools prepared students for college, and college prepared students to be cultured members of the leisure class. But as the American school system expanded, public high schools were pressured by industry and by parents to train students for jobs. This resulted in the construction of two types of high schools: vocational and general (college preparatory). Today, in most areas, one high school offers both types of programs. Vocational courses such as typing, stenography, and mechanical drawing are commonplace in the high school curriculum. Colleges and universities have also become even more involved in vocational and professional training. Today's college student usually pursues two academic goals at the same time: he increases his general knowledge while preparing for a specific career.

In helping to educate a student for adult work and adult life, American schools strive, above all, to be practical. John Dewey's philosophy, which claims that the only worthwhile knowledge is knowledge that can be used, has greatly influenced American educators. They do not want to teach useless facts which will quickly be forgotten; they want to teach attitudes and skills which will help produce useful, responsible, happy adults. No longer are educators content to teach just reading, writing, and arithmetic. Typical grammar school and high school programs now include science, social studies, art, music, and sports—subjects which help students live in the world with greater understanding and enjoyment. In the years ahead, more labor-saving devices will allow adults to do household chores more quickly and easily. More automation will probably lead to a shorter work week for most workers. Leisure time will increase for working adults and, as life expectancy increases, more Americans will spend more years as retired, elderly people. The schools, therefore, have a new obligation: to educate for productive use of leisure time.

Modern educators also feel that the school must fill important educational gaps left by the home. Therefore, it is not uncommon for the curriculum to include a campaign against cigarette smoking, a course in driving an automobile, cooking and sewing classes, advice on hygiene and grooming, and sex education. Schools consider it their job to educate the whole child, his mind and his body, his intellect and his emotions, to cope successfully with adult responsibilities as wage earners, parents, and citizens.

Dewey also influenced teaching techniques. Education must be meaningful and children learn best by doing—these are the basic tenets of progressive education. Thus, science is taught largely through student experimentation; the study of music involves making music; democratic principles are put into practice in the student council; group projects involving student leadership encourage creativity, individual initiative, and teamwork.

How well-educated is the American public? About 60 percent of American adults are high school graduates. By 1980, it is predicted that 85 percent of teen-agers will graduate high school. The number of Americans attending and completing college is also growing rapidly, especially among minority groups such as blacks and Spanish-speaking people.

The quality as well as the quantity of American education seems to be improving. Tests seem to indicate that children educated during the 1960s learned more than the students of the 1950s. In colleges, too, the quality of education is improving, even though higher education is now mass education. In fact, some educators believe that the improvement may be because colleges and universities can be more selective now that they have a larger pool of talent to draw from. Academic achievement on the highest level—that of creative scholarship—has also advanced in recent years. In 1930, only 5 percent of Nobel Prizes were held by Americans; today the figure exceeds 40 percent. In 1971, the Commissioner of Education wrote, "We know that ours is the greatest educational system ever devised by man. But it falls short of our aspirations. We must improve it."

The Commissioner admitted that the American educational system has "great voids in its capacity to satisfy the pressing requirements of our people." What's wrong and why? This is a difficult question to answer briefly because in recent years almost every aspect of education has been scrutinized and criticized. Schools are often scoffed at for the insipid and inadequate training they provide. In inner-city schools populated largely by minority groups, students and parents have accused many principals of being unsympathetic to the needs of the community. Teachers are frequently criticized for having a middle-class bias that makes them ineffective with students from low-income families. School facilities are clearly unequal; they are of much better quality in the richer suburban school districts than in the city schools. Progressive educators criticize the old-fashioned classroom setup, still used in many schools, that forces children to sit silently in neat rows of desks for several hours a day. Textbooks have been much maligned—basic readers for depicting a middle-class world that children living in the slums cannot identify with; and social studies books for misrepresenting certain groups such as blacks, Indians, and women. The question of what should and what should not be discussed in schools is under endless debate. Should schools teach black history and sex education? Is the study of American history being used for political indoctrination? Are teachers cowardly about allowing students to debate controversial issues? Students, too, have been criticized for their rejection of authority and for the widespread use of illegal drugs.

The quality of life within many schools leaves much to be desired. This was brought to public attention during the 1960s, when student discontent resulted in organized protests on many college campuses and in many high schools. During the 1970s organized expressions of discontent have been less frequent and less serious, perhaps because student demands for a greater voice in school administration have been at least partially met.

The quality of learning in American schools has been attacked in at least one major area: that of language skills. A recent study revealed that 30 to 50 percent of students entering junior college need reading help. Also, among today's high school and college students, there is a noticeable lack of writing skill.

Inner-city schools are perhaps the least effective institutions in our educational system. Admittedly, the children attending these schools are harder to teach for a variety of reasons. The flight of white, middle-class families to the suburbs left big city public schools with mostly lower-income students from minority groups. Many are deprived children from impoverished homes with only one parent. Many come to school ill-prepared and poorly motivated to learn. A large number are bilingual and need help in learning English. In addition, inner-city students often change residences and therefore often change schools. A changing classroom population is difficult to teach. To cope with all these difficulties, inner-city schools need better facilities, extra staff, and many special programs. In recent years, educators have tried many new approaches to help inner-city children learn more. Federally funded programs for disadvantaged pre-schoolers have been established. Bilingual teachers have been employed to instruct the foreign-born. Alternative schools have been established for high school students who prefer a combination work-study program and for those who learn better in a more casual, intimate environment than the traditional classroom can provide. Unfortunately, the money is not always available to maintain programs that have proved successful with inner-city children.

The monetary problem, in fact, is the most serious problem facing American education. Teachers demand higher salaries, equipment and maintenance costs rise, and the schools need more money. But taxpayers in many cities have voted down proposals for increased property taxes to supply the schools with additional funds. Several school systems have been on the brink of closing because they couldn't pay their bills. In some cities, the school year has been cut short by a few days or weeks because of insufficient funds. The widespread school financial crisis suggests that the nation needs a new approach to school financing, giving school districts greater support from the state and federal governments.

All these problems cannot be underestimated; yet American education also deserves credit for its remarkable accomplishments. Our educational system surpasses almost every nation's in teaching basic academic skills to nearly everyone and offering unlimited educational opportunity to those who are capable of advanced studies. Despite its deficiencies, American education provides a firm foundation upon which American democracy is built.

EXERCISES

Comprehension. Choose the correct answer.

1. Most American children are educated in
   (a) private schools.
   (b) free public schools.
   (c) parochial schools.

2. All American children must attend school until they are
   (a) 10 years old.
   (b) 18 years old.
   (c) 16 years old.

3. American public schools are controlled
   (a) by the federal government.
   (b) by the state government.

(c) by the local school board.

4. Private schools charge
   (a) tuition.
   (b) taxes.
   (c) credit.

5. Schools operated by a religious denomination
   (a) are supported in part by tuition fees.
   (b) are controlled by the government.
   (c) are totally supported by the state.

6. The doctrine of the separation of church and state is part of the
   (a) Emancipation Proclamation.
   (b) Constitution.
   (c) Declaration of Independence.

7. What percentage of American teen-agers finish high school?
   (a) 40 percent
   (b) 60 percent
   (c) 80 percent

8. American schools have serious problems because of
   (a) insufficient students.
   (b) insufficient teachers.
   (c) insufficient funds.

9. A philosopher who had a great influence on American education was
   (a) Santayana.
   (b) Spencer.
   (c) Dewey.

10. American teachers believe that students learn best by
    (a) doing.
    (b) listening.
    (c) repeating.

Vocabulary and Usage. Give the meaning of each of the following words. Use each in a sentence.

obligation	bilingual	parochial
entrust	guarantee	tenet
fund	prediction	insipid
gap	cope	bias
pace	investment	impoverished

Conversation and Discussion. Discuss the importance of education in your life.

XIX
Religion in American Life

Diversity—that is the dominant characteristic of religion in the United States. Although Christianity has always been the major American faith, the existence of more than 250 different religious sects here has forced Americans to be tolerant of all forms of worship—Christian and non-Christian.

Many immigrants came to the American colonies to escape religious persecution. Therefore, it was natural that the nation's founders demanded legal guarantees of religious freedom. The First Amendment to the Constitution forbids the establishment of an official national religion and prohibits governmental subsidies to religious groups. It also prohibits state or federal interference with religious institutions or practices. Americans are free to practice or not to practice religion, whichever they choose.

Although the American government is free from religious influences, references to God are a part of many official customs and acts. "We are a religious people whose institutions presuppose a Supreme Being," said U.S. Supreme Court Justice William O. Douglas. For example, sessions of Congress and state legislatures begin with prayers. Our national motto is "In God We Trust," and our pledge of allegiance to the flag declares that this is "one nation under God."

When the American census is taken (every ten years), people are not asked about religious identification. Therefore, the only exact figures on American religious participation come from churches and synagogues which compile statistics on members. However, many Americans who consider themselves part of a particular religious body do not maintain church membership. About 60 percent of Americans are affiliated with a particular church or synagogue. Of these, about 95 percent are Christians and nearly 5 percent are Jews. Only a small number of Americans belong to other faiths. Approximately 58 percent of church-affiliated Christians are Protestants (about 72 million people). American Protestantism is divided into more than 200 different denominations, most of them with fewer than 50,000 members. Only about twenty-two Protestant sects claim a membership as large as 500,000. The major Protestant bodies, all having memberships in the millions, are the United Methodists, Baptists, Lutherans, Presbyterians, and Episcopalians.

Two interesting Protestant sects founded in the United States are the Mormons and the Christian Scientists. The Mormons (officially known as the Church of Jesus Christ of Latter-day Saints) were organized in New York in 1830. Because they practiced polygamy (plural marriage), they were forced out of several established communities. So they traveled westward and settled in the unpopulated valley of the Great Salt Lake, where they built a thriving community. Then the federal government passed antipolygamy laws and refused to admit Utah as a state until 1896, after the Mormons had discontinued this practice. Today, there are two million Mormons in the U.S.A. Most of them live in Utah and in eastern Idaho, where they are the dominant religious sect, but many reside in other western states.

The Christian Science Church was founded by Mary Baker Eddy in 1879. Christian Scientists believe that since man is wholly spiritual, healing of sickness results from spiritual understanding rather than from medical treatment. The Christian Science movement now has more than 3,300 churches and societies in at least forty-six countries, but about two-thirds of these are within the United States. The organization maintains reading rooms in many cities. Its newspaper, the *Christian Science Monitor,* is considered one of the world's finest newspapers.

The combined Protestant sects form the largest religious faith in the United States. But Roman Catholicism is by far the largest unified religious body. About 48 million Americans are baptized members of Catholic congregations. Since many Catholics send their children to parochial schools, Catholic funds have built thousands of elementary and secondary schools, plus many fine colleges and universities. Catholics have also played a prominent role in American politics, although it was not until 1960, when John F. Kennedy was elected President, that a Catholic held the highest office in the land.

The third major religion in the United States is Judaism. Nearly 6 million Americans are members of Jewish congregations. There are three major denominations in Judaism: Orthodox, Conservative, and Reform. During the Sabbath, which is observed from sundown Friday until sundown Saturday, Orthodox Jews do not ride or conduct business. Jewish tradition imposes certain dietary restrictions, prohibiting pork and certain seafoods and forbidding the serving of milk products at meals which include meat or poultry. Reform Judaism does not impose these restrictions.

How potent a force is religion in the United States today? Because it provides individuals and families with an identity and a social sphere, religion plays a large role in the lives of many Americans. But in terms of influencing behavior and philosophical outlook, religion has declined in importance.

Identification with a religious group gives the individual a feeling of belonging and a sure, clear place within the otherwise impersonal urban community. Social groups, close friendships, and marriages are usually formed with members of one's own religion. As elsewhere, in the United States religion provides the customs and ceremonies that mark life's most important events—birth, coming of age, marriage, and death. But American churches and synagogues are not only places where prayers are recited and ceremonies are conducted; they are also community centers where educational, cultural, social, and philanthropic activities are held.

Perhaps because religion is an important social force, religious affiliation has increased greatly during the 20th century. In 1910, 43 percent of the population were members of churches, compared with the 1972 figure of 60 percent. However, other statistics indicate that religion is actually losing its hold upon Americans. For one thing, church attendance has declined in recent years. In 1958, in a typical week, religious services were attended by 49 percent of Americans; in 1972, the figure was 40 percent. In a recent survey conducted by a popular family magazine, readers were asked, "Is religion losing its influence on family life today?" Eighty-five percent answered yes. When Americans need personal advice, they are frequently turning to psychiatrists or to professional counselors rather than to religious leaders. The twentieth century has often been called a secular age, and certainly it is in the U.S.A. Belief in a personal God, concern for God's judgment of one's behavior, and concern about the afterlife seem to be declining.

The modern American seems less worried about saving his soul for the hereafter and more interested in improving his life on earth. In this endeavor, Americans have a strong faith in their ability to improve conditions through their own efforts. Ben Franklin said, "God helps them that help themselves." During World War II, the same idea was expressed as "Praise the Lord and pass the ammunition." In other words, Americans do not believe in passively accepting whatever seems to be God's will; they count upon their own initiative to get what they want.

Of course, generalizations about religious attitudes can be misleading because religious outlook varies quite a bit depending upon one's age group, social class, degree of education, and region of the country. Religion probably exercises a greater control over the behavior of Catholics than of Protestants or Jews. The rising rate of interfaith marriages suggests that religious differences are less significant to this generation of young adults than to their parents' generation. Religion seems to have a greater emotional grip upon the poor and uneducated than upon the affluent and educated. In the southern part of the country, often called the *Bible Belt*, parishioners are generally more traditional in their attitudes toward religion than is the rest of the nation.

A discussion of religion in the United States would be incomplete without mention of an interesting development which began in the late 1960s and has continued into the 1970s. Running counter to the general national trend of declining interest in religion, a resurging religious interest has evolved among youth. A 1971 study of college students revealed that undergraduate courses in religion are drawing many more students than in past years and that religion is the fastest-growing field of study in secular universities. The most conspicuous of the young religious zealots are commonly called "Jesus people." Their life-style—involving long hair, beads, opposition to drugs, Gospel "rock" music, evangelism, and Bible study—has introduced a new religious approach. In fact, two "rock" musical versions of the life of Christ (performed mostly by unknown entertainers in their teens and twenties) have toured the nation, appearing before large, enthusiastic audiences.

Probably influenced by the nontraditional religious fervor of the young, people in churches and synagogues throughout the nation are now creating new kinds of religious services. They are using popular media of expression—jazz, "rock," and folk music; folk dancing and modern dancing; contemporary art and poetry; even plays, slides, and movies. These new services have offended some traditionalists. One angry parishioner, after watching a "rock" music group perform in his church, indignantly asked the priest, "What do you think this is—a nightclub?" But many congregations respond enthusiastically to the discovery that prayer need not be just mindless repetition of words and music from past centuries. In fact, many of these progressive institutions draw capacity crowds to their weekly services, while more traditional places of worship are half-empty.

Considering the history of bloodshed that religious differences have wrought elsewhere, Americans can be proud of the degree of religious tolerance which exists in their country. Members of small minority groups may, in some areas of the country, find themselves handicapped in winning acceptance professionally and socially. But religious prejudice is much less prevalent now than it was a few decades ago. Barriers between various faiths seem to be lowering. When American attitudes toward racial minorities become as liberal as current attitudes toward religious minorities, the United States will have taken another big step toward the realization of its ideals.

EXERCISES

Comprehension. Choose the correct answer.

1. The major characteristic of religion in America is
   (a) attendance.
   (b) diversity.
   (c) unanimity.

2. American government is
   (a) Christian.
   (b) free from religious influence.
   (c) opposed to religion.

3. Two interesting religions which began in the United States are
   (a) Judaism and Deism.
   (b) Christian Science and Mormonism.
   (c) Deism and Christian Science.
4. Most Mormons live in
   (a) New York.
   (b) Utah and Idaho.
   (c) California.
5. Mary Baker Eddy founded
   (a) Deism.
   (b) Mormonism.
   (c) Christian Science.
6. Most Americans are
   (a) Christians.
   (b) Jews.
   (c) Mormons.
7. The single largest unified religious body in the United States is
   (a) the Presbyterian Church.
   (b) the Roman Catholic Church.
   (c) the Baptist Church.
8. President Kennedy was a
   (a) Jew.
   (b) Presbyterian.
   (c) Catholic.
9. Religion, as an influence on most Americans, is
   (a) declining.
   (b) increasing.
   (c) remaining the same.
10. Religious tolerance in the United States seems to be
   (a) declining.
   (b) increasing.
   (c) remaining the same.

Vocabulary and Usage. Give the meaning of each of the following words. Use each in a sentence.

dominant	escape
motto	stress
sect	thrive
potent	secular
statistics	influence

Conversation and Discussion. What effect has religious tolerance had on American history?

XX
News and Entertainment Media

Americans spend about five hours each day in leisure activities. Those who live in or near large cities spend some of this time at theaters, opera houses, night clubs, zoos, and museums. Americans who live in rural areas do not usually have such places to visit, but, like urban residents, they can enjoy the most popular sources of information and entertainment: radio, television, movies, books, magazines, and newspapers.

RADIO

Almost every American family owns at least one radio, and many have three or four. Years ago, families gathered around one big living room radio. Today, people take small, lightweight radios with them into the bedroom (clock radios), down the street (transistor radios), on the road (car radios), and into the cornfields (radios built into tractors). Radios have even been built into hair dryers and sunglasses!

Since the development of television, radio is no longer the major source of home entertainment; but Americans still turn to radio when they want the latest news quickly. Many stations broadcast up-to-the-minute news every half-hour. Americans tend to listen to radio for short periods. In an effort to hold audiences, many radio stations appeal to special interests. Some offer an all-news or all-music format; others broadcast professional sporting events. In large cities, some stations attract immigrants by presenting foreign-language programs. One New York City station broadcasts in thirteen languages!

There are two types of radio broadcasting—AM and FM. FM can produce a wider range of sounds and can also broadcast in stereophonic sound. In recent years, FM has become increasingly popular. Many radios are equipped to receive both AM and FM.

TELEVISION

Television was in its infancy in 1946, but by the 1950s it was a firmly established industry. Today, there are about 99 million TV sets in the United States; 99 percent of American households have at least one set, and 54 percent have two or more. Color TV is in 60 percent of American homes. The average American between his second and sixty-fifth year spends 3,000 entire days (almost nine years of his life!) watching TV.

In the United States, there is no government-owned television network. Commercial television attempts to please a vast audience of all age groups and educational levels by presenting entertainment that can be understood by all. Many adults are annoyed by the simplicity and triteness of most TV shows; they call the TV set the "idiot box" or the "boob tube." A typical day's TV listing includes cartoons and other children's shows, family situation comedies, news and weather, mysteries, westerns, melodramatic serials, interview shows, sports, movies, and musical reviews.

"Public" television stations offer a wide variety of high-quality entertainment and information without the annoying interruptions of commercials. Funds to operate public TV come from donations by individuals and industries and, to a small degree, from the government. Public television has been highly praised for imaginative, appealing shows which help children learn basic reading concepts, valuable psychological insights, English, and Spanish. Fine dramatic and musical presentations, award-winning movies, and intelligent discussions of national problems often take up the evening hours on public TV. For those who seek self-improvement via TV, there are "how-to" shows (daytime and evening) which teach cooking, skiing, sewing, guitar-playing, yoga, and dozens of other skills. Also offered are college courses which give academic credit to enrolled listeners.

MOVIES

Most American movies are produced in Hollywood, California. Hollywood, which is actually not a separate city but a part of Los Angeles, is an ideal spot for the movie industry. The sun shines most of the time, and the climate is mild. Almost every kind of natural scenery is within a few hours' drive.

Hollywood becomes the center of national attention one evening a year—Academy Award night. At the Academy Award presentations held each spring, statuettes called *Oscars* are given to film industry winners in dozens of categories, including best actor, best actress, and best picture. The winners are chosen by members of the industry before the ceremony, but their names are kept secret until presentation night, when they are announced in a long, nationally televised program.

Motion pictures were extremely popular in the United States until after World War II, when television captured much of the movie audience. Geared to the masses, Hollywood movies offered much the same type of entertainment as television. With free entertainment in their homes, many Americans simply stopped going to movies. Between 1946 and 1956, movie attendance was cut in half. At the same time, production costs zoomed. The movie industry was in trouble.

The industry adjusted in a number of ways. Movie companies rented sound stages to TV companies and sold old movies to TV. To cut costs, Hollywood produced fewer movies and filmed many of them overseas. To lure audiences, the industry invested in new lenses, wider screens, and stereophonic sound. Studios also began producing kinds of entertainment that could not be offered by TV—films with controversial or shocking themes, films with huge casts and lavish settings. As a result of these changes, today the American motion picture industry is thriving.

BOOKS

American publishers sell more than a billion hardcover and paperback books annually. Every year the publishing industry prints more than 25,000 new titles and about 12,000 new editions of previously published books. More than 1,000 different titles a year are published in many areas of general interest (such as fiction, travel, books for children, and biographies) and in many areas of special interest (including science, sociology, economics, history, medicine, technology, literary studies, and education). Including books printed by the federal government and by university presses, some 80,000 titles are published each year.

MAGAZINES

Thousands of different magazines are published in this country each month. Some appeal to the general public, others to special groups. The major news magazines —*Time*, *Newsweek*, and *U.S. News & World Report*— reach a combined weekly readership of nearly 7 million. Also popular are monthly women's magazines such as *McCall's*, *Ladies' Home Journal*, and *Good Housekeeping*. Each of the six leaders in this field has a circulation between 4 and 8 million. About 16 million copies of *TV Guide* are sold each week.

Many magazines are aimed at occupational groups such as farmers, teachers, and doctors. Dozens of children's magazines are published, including comic books (magazines that present stories in comic strip form). There are magazines about hobbies such as photography, hunting, fishing, and sewing. There are magazines filled with photographs and stories about famous entertainers. Every major religious group sponsors at least one magazine, as do many industries.

Digest magazines consist largely of articles reprinted from other publications. *Reader's Digest* is the most popular monthly magazine published in this country; more than 17 million copies are sold every month.

NEWSPAPERS

In the United States, about 62 million newspapers are sold every day. An additional 49 million are sold each Sunday. In addition to news, newspapers contain stock market reports, sports coverage, fashions, recipes, want ads, medical information, and advice on child care. Most daily papers also include television listings, movie and TV reviews, and chess and bridge columns.

To many readers, the most entertaining part of the paper is the "funny page" or comic section. Comics have been called "America's favorite form of fiction." About 100 million Americans read them each day—more than those who read any other section of the newspaper. Almost everyone can find a comic strip that will appeal to him, whether his taste is for slapstick humor, melodrama, violence, adventure, or intellectual satire. Many portray characters with which readers can identify—such as career girls, professional men, and harried parents.

Comics often present real problems in humorous parables. In *Peanuts,* for example, the main character is a likable kid named Charlie Brown, who is constantly perplexed and defeated by everyday situations. Some of the attitudes prevalent in the United States are reflected in an exaggerated form in comic strips. *Blondie,* for example, exaggerates the concept of the emancipated, superior American woman. Blondie is efficient and smart; her husband, although he tries hard, is weak and incompetent, both at home and at work. *Dennis the Menace,* a cocky kindergartner, terrorizes and outsmarts his family, his teacher, and his neighbors, satirizing what some have called a child-dominated culture.

American comics are translated into many languages and represent one of our most influential exports. They reach more than 200 million people in some sixty foreign countries.

* * *

Technological advances have made mass communication inexpensive and immediately available to everyone. Americans spend more time absorbing the products of the mass communications media than in any other activity except working and sleeping. As a result, Americans are probably among the best informed people in the world; yet we are not as well-informed as we might be. Concerning public affairs, Americans do not always know "the whole truth and nothing but the truth."

The public itself is partly at fault. Americans turn to the mass communications media for entertainment more often than for information. On an average weekday, 77 percent of American adults read the daily newspaper. But more of them read the comics than the editorials. During an entire evening of TV viewing, most Americans spend only about fifteen minutes with the news. According to one newspaper columnist, 80 percent of adults in the United States know very little about foreign affairs.

But what of the concerned adult who wants to know what's happening in the world and why? Can he get the truth from the mass communications media? To some extent that depends upon how long and how far he looks, since every form of mass communication is influenced by certain forces. Book publishers, for example, publish what they think will sell. This means that an exaggerated, alarming, attention-getting exposé may appear in print while a high-quality novel or book of poetry by an unknown author is likely to remain unpublished.

The communications media are, generally, private businesses operated for profit. What newspapers, magazines, radio, and TV present to the public is largely influenced by three factors—the owners' opinions, the advertisers' best interests, and the attitudes of the public (as the media interpret them).

The press is traditionally supposed to be the "watchdog" of government. In other words, we depend upon dedicated reporters to sniff out unethical or illegal behavior by public officials and expose these evils to the public. On the whole, the press performs this job well. But, like all people, reporters, publishers, and station owners have biases of their own. These sometimes influence the selection and tone of news coverage. In fact, most newspapers commonly identify themselves with one of the two major political parties.

The mass communications media compete for advertising dollars and public attention. Therefore, any publication or broadcasting station is likely to ignore or minimize a news item that would harm one of its advertisers. For example, when Ralph Nader wrote a book attacking the American automobile industry for producing unsafe cars, magazines that sold advertising to automobile manufacturers did not want to mention the book.

Since industries prefer to advertise where they will reach the largest number of potential customers, the newspapers, magazines, and broadcasting stations do everything they can to hold the largest audience possible. On commercial TV, this goal leads to a great deal of sports coverage and generally inadequate analysis of the national and international situation. It also means very little opera, classical music, or Shakespearean drama, and a great deal of unsophisticated comedy. Generally, the mass communications media try to please the public by reinforcing popular and traditional ideas rather than helping the public to understand (or, at least, accept) new ideas.

It would be naive to think that news coverage in the United States is always "the whole truth and nothing but the truth." However, the concerned citizen who exposes himself to a wide variety of publications and broadcasting stations can obtain a reasonably accurate picture of what's happening in the world. The United States government cannot control the news and entertainment media except to protect the public. It can prohibit misleading advertising and ban the sale of obscene material, but it cannot censor news. Public officials sometimes withhold information concerning governmental activities from the news media. Attempts to do this, however, are often exposed by persistent reporters.

The constitutional guarantee of freedom of expression allows writers, news commentators, and public figures to state their opinions openly, without fear of governmental reprisal. No official power is controlling what is said to the public. No particular point of view is forced upon the news media. No American need be ignorant about public affairs in this nation where freedom of speech makes a wide range of events and ideas available to the public.

EXERCISES

Comprehension. Choose the correct answer.

1. Television first became popular nationally in the
   (a) sixties.
   (b) fifties.
   (c) thirties.

2. TV sets can be found in
   (a) 99 percent of American homes.
   (b) 75 percent of American homes.
   (c) 50 percent of American homes.
3. TV networks in the United States are owned
   (a) by the government.
   (b) privately.
   (c) federally.
4. TV is sometimes referred to as the
   (a) cartoon.
   (b) media.
   (c) idiot box.
5. Most American movies are produced in
   (a) Hollywood.
   (b) New York.
   (c) Buffalo.
6. The prize offered by the film industry to the best motion picture of the year is called
   (a) an Emmy.
   (b) an Oscar.
   (c) a Citation.
7. The most popular magazine published in the United States is called
   (a) *Time*.
   (b) *TV Guide*.
   (c) *Reader's Digest*.
8. A famous comic strip which exaggerates the American child-dominated culture is called
   (a) *Blondie*.
   (b) *Dennis the Menace*.
   (c) *Peanuts*.
9. On an average weekday, a daily newspaper is read by
   (a) 47 percent of American adults.
   (b) 77 percent of American adults.
   (c) 87 percent of American adults.

10. Freedom of expression is guaranteed by the
    (a) Declaration of Independence.
    (b) Constitution.
    (c) President.

Vocabulary and Usage. Give the meaning of each of the following words. Use each in a sentence.

leisure	press
melodrama	audience
transistor	bias
advertise	media
commercial	cartoon

Conversation and Discussion. Explain why it is better if the government does not control the news media. Why is it important to be informed?

XXI
Sports for Spectators and Participants

Most Americans enjoy athletics both as participants and spectators. Winter and summer sports, outdoor and indoor sports, individual and team sports, competitive and non-competitive sports—all have a good following. Americans have adopted and sometimes modified many sports which originated elsewhere. Because of our diversified climate and geography, any sport that was brought here by an immigrant group found a suitable environment. However, some of the nation's favorite team sports originated here.

The athletic interests of American children are strongly encouraged by parents and schools. Most parents help their youngsters learn to ride a bike or play ball. Children commonly receive private or group instruction in popular sports such as swimming, tennis, and ice-skating. School athletic programs generally begin in the elementary grades and introduce students to gymnastic skills and popular team sports such as basketball, volleyball, and softball (a modification of baseball played with a larger and softer ball).

For youngsters in the higher elementary grades, many schools organize teams that compete against other schools for a league championship. Also, many communities organize children and adolescents into teams that play for city, state, and perhaps even national championships.

For high school and college students, there is great emphasis upon competitive athletics. The term *intramural sports* refers to competition among students of the same school or college. *Intercollegiate* competition (contests involving teams or individuals from different schools) is often well attended by students, alumni, and community residents. Intercollegiate football attracts more attention and TV coverage than any other college sport.

Much can be said in favor of the American emphasis upon athletics. Physical education programs promote good health and body development. Team games teach youngsters to work together cooperatively and practice good sportsmanship. However, the highly competitive nature of school and community athletics—the importance of winning—sometimes puts great pressure upon the youngster who is a good player and makes the child who is not a superior athlete feel that he is not welcome to participate.

Because competitive athletics is followed so avidly by so many Americans, outstanding athletes (amateur and professional) become national celebrities. Their names and faces become familiar to large numbers of people. Their professional achievements and personal problems become household discussions. They are sought after by advertisers to endorse products, and they often appear on TV selling razor blades, deodorants, cereals, and other items. Some outstanding athletes earn $100,000 or more per year in salaries from their teams or in prize money; and many earn additional sums for endorsing products, appearing on TV "talk" shows, or writing. American youngsters, hearing about the high incomes and glamorous lives of the nation's famous athletes, yearn to follow in their footsteps. As a result, many youngsters take athletics more seriously than they should.

However, the fact that outstanding athletes become national heroes has been beneficial in one respect. The large representation of blacks among the nation's most idolized sports figures has been a positive force in molding the racial attitudes of the young.

Competitive athletics is serious business to professionals and to amateurs with top standing. But the same sports that are important pursuits for the experts are also enjoyed by large numbers of moderately skilled Americans who dabble in the activities mostly for fun and exercise.

In the United States, the fastest growing participant sport of the 1970s is tennis. Tennis was once considered the pastime of the rich, who played on courts in their exclusive country clubs or on their own estates. But in recent years the game has become democratized; millions of Americans of every age, class, and color have taken up the sport. The number of outdoor courts is increasing at the rate of 4,600 a year—about 13 new courts per day! In addition, the country now has about 500 indoor courts, making tennis a year-round activity even in colder areas. There are now about 11 million tennis players in the United States, nearly double the number of ten years ago.

Why this sudden increase in the popularity of tennis? There are two likely reasons. One is the growing public interest in big-time tournament tennis, which TV has brought into the home. The other is the growing national concern with physical fitness, which is attracting people to the more vigorous sports. Also, tennis is a fine family activity, since a doubles game can accommodate the typical four-member American family.

Cycling is another sport that has enjoyed phenomenal growth within the past ten years. Bike-riding was once considered a sport for children. Now it provides exercise, recreation, and transportation for adults as well. In 1969, only 12 percent of bikes purchased were for adult use. In 1972, about 50 percent were for adults. Growing traffic problems and national concern with pollution may account for some of this booming interest in bikes. During nice weather, many urban adults can be seen pedaling their way to work, thus avoiding the trouble and expense of parking a car in a downtown parking lot. Cycling trips for recreational touring are growing in popularity for families, classes, clubs, and other groups. Many communities are expanding their bike routes and other services to cyclers in order to accommodate the growing number of riders. Bike sales were nearly 9 million in 1971, nearly 14 million in 1972, and estimated at 15 million for 1973. In 1973, about 83 million Americans used a bike, and experts predict that by 1975 about half the population will be bike-riders.

Golf is another sport that keeps growing more popular each year. From 1950 to 1971, participation grew from 3 million to about 12 million. Played during warmer weather, golf is one of the favorite sports of the middle-aged, since it provides fresh air, sunshine, and exercise that is not extremely strenuous.

Indoor sports are also widely enjoyed. Thousands of gymnasiums and indoor swimming pools are to be found throughout the country. There are also many skating rinks and bowling alleys.

Bowling is both an individual and a team sport. It was introduced into the United States by the original Dutch settlers of New Amsterdam (the site which is now New York City). Ninepins, as the game was then known, was modified by the addition of a tenth pin. When these pins were later set up in a triangle, the modern bowling game was created.

More adults participate in bowling than in any other competitive sport. About one out of every ten adult Americans plays regularly with a team or league. Frequently, bowling leagues are formed by men (or women) who work together or belong to the same church or social club. Leagues usually bowl once a week during autumn, winter, and spring.

Winter sports such as skiing, ice-skating, snowmobiling, and ice-fishing are quite popular, especially in the northern and western mountain states. Hockey (the common American name for ice hockey) is played by many youngsters living in colder areas. The national sport of Canada, hockey is also a popular spectator sport in the United

States. Many American cities have hockey teams that compete along with Canadian teams for the coveted Stanley Cup. Hockey is a fast, exciting game involving two six-man teams on an ice-covered rink. Each team tries to hit a hard rubber disk (called a *puck*) into the other team's goal or cage.

The United States has approximately 88,600 miles of seacoast, five large freshwater inland seas called the Great Lakes, tens of thousands of smaller lakes, and countless rivers. As a result, millions of Americans participate in water sports such as swimming, surfing, diving, sailing, powerboating, and waterskiing. In 1971, more than 32 million fishing licenses were issued. Deep-sea fishing is popular with Americans who live or vacation along the ocean coastlines.

Hunting is permitted in some national and state parks as well as on some private lands. Americans purchase more than 22 million hunting licenses annually. The United States has a wide variety of game animals ranging from the Kodiak bear (the world's largest carnivore) to rabbits and ground squirrels. Game birds include pheasant, grouse, ducks, and geese. Almost all game is protected by law and may be hunted in limited numbers during certain seasons only.

Many kinds of spectator sports are popular in the United States. Horse racing, dog racing, and automobile racing rank among the nation's favorites. Nearly 7 billion dollars is bet annually by spectators at horse and dog racing tracks. Boxing and wrestling matches are also well attended. Most world championship boxing matches, especially in the heavier weight classes, have been fought in the United States.

Three of the nation's most popular team participation

sports—baseball, football, and basketball—are also spectator events. Although these three games are played by most schoolboys, they have reached their highest development in organized teams of professional athletes.

According to popular tradition, baseball was invented in Cooperstown, New York in 1839. Whatever its origin, the game is now a distinctly American institution. The sport is played with a wooden club called a bat and a hard, round, leather-covered ball. The players on each team take turns trying to hit the ball with the bat. The batter swings at the ball after it has been thrown toward him by the other team's pitcher. In professional games, the pitched ball sometimes travels faster than 100 miles per hour, so protective helmets are worn by all players when "at bat." When playing a defensive position, each player wears a large leather glove to protect his hand from batted or thrown balls.

Baseball is played on a flat field, a portion of which is called the *diamond.* At the four corners of the diamond (which is really a square measuring ninety feet on each side) are four bases called *first, second, third,* and *home plate.* Standing at home plate, the batter tries to hit the baseball with the bat and then run counterclockwise around the diamond, touching all the bases in order, while the other team chases the ball. When a player reaches home plate before the ball does, he has scored a *point* or *run.* If a player hits the ball across the field into the spectators' seats or out of the ballpark, he has hit a *home run.*

A normal baseball game takes about two hours to play. On Sunday afternoons and holidays, teams usually play two games *(a doubleheader).* On pleasant summer afternoons, families by the hundreds of thousands crowd the nation's ballparks to enjoy the fresh air, hot dogs, and the ball games. Most ballparks have installed lights for night games so that working people can see baseball during the week.

An indication of baseball's popularity is the fact that American English contains many expressions taken from the game. *He has two strikes against him* means that he is at a disadvantage before he starts to do something. *A foul ball* is someone who is disliked or considered incompetent. *He is off base* means he is impertinent. *I'll take a rain check* is the same as saying, "I can't come now, but I will gladly accept your invitation for another time." (Rain checks are given at all baseball games. They permit ticket-holders free entrance to another game if the game they paid to see is halted by bad weather before it is half over.)

Since the mid-nineteenth century, when baseball was first played as an organized sport, its audience has grown rapidly, along with the nation's soaring population. For many years, it has been called the national sport. Every season about 30 million people go to ballparks to watch baseball games in the two major professional leagues —the American League and the National League—and millions more watch on TV. In each of the two major leagues there is an Eastern and a Western Division, and each division has six teams. At the end of the season, the two divisional winners in each league play each other in a five-game series. These two matches determine the pennant winners, who then play each other in the seven-game World Series. The World Series, played in the fall, is the most popular sporting attraction in the United States.

Yet even before the final pitch of the baseball season has been thrown, the American male's thoughts turn from the baseball diamond to the football field. American football is not the same game as soccer, which is called football in other parts of the world. However, both games probably developed from primitive sports in which players kicked a ball.

Football is played with a ball that is approximately oval. The football field is 120 yards long and 160 feet wide. The length of the field is marked by lines every five yards. The first ten yards at each end of the field are called end zones. Each end zone contains two goal posts connected by a horizontal bar ten feet off the ground. The object of the game is either to carry the ball into the other team's end zone without being knocked to the ground or to kick the ball between the other team's goal posts. Football is a rugged sport involving much physical contact between players. But there are rules prohibiting certain conduct likely to lead to injuries, and a team is penalized if a player breaks any of the rules. Also, to prevent injuries, players wear protective clothing—helmets, cleated shoes, and thick padding. Nevertheless, football players do get hurt, but far less often than one would suppose from watching the game.

Every year about 41 million people attend professional and college football games. Many more attend high school games and watch professional and intercollegiate contests on television. The football season extends from early autumn into winter, and the game is played in fair or foul weather.

Like baseball and football, basketball is played by amateur school teams (from grammar school on up) and by professional teams. Altogether, the game is played and watched by more people than any other sport in the United States. The first game of basketball was played in Massachusetts in 1891 when Dr. James Naismith attached two fruit baskets high on the walls at both ends of a gymnasium. The object of the game was, and still is, to throw a large round ball into the opposing team's basket and to prevent this from being done to your own team's basket. Height is a great advantage, so tall boys especially may harbor dreams of careers as professional basketball players. But nearly every youngster enjoys trying to "make a basket." As a result, backboards for practice shooting are standard equipment in playgrounds and back yards and above garage doors.

In recent years, American interest in all kinds of athletics has greatly increased. Spectator sports are growing in popularity because Americans have more leisure time to watch them and because TV gives so many athletic events nationwide exposure. Today, women probably constitute a larger percentage of sports enthusiasts than ever before. And, thanks to TV, children are learning to understand and enjoy games like baseball and football at a very early age.

About 60 million men and women (55 percent of the nation's adult population) fit twenty-five minutes of exercise into their schedules at least three times a week. Most Americans have spare time for sports and extra money for equipment and instruction. And they can justify their bowling, golf, or tennis expenses as a necessary aid to keeping physically fit. Many adults who have no interest in athletic games prefer to keep in condition by following a regular program of calisthenics, perhaps one that has been published in a paperback book or is conducted regularly on TV. Yoga, isometrics, and aerobics are all popular with both men and women. Walking is the major form of exercise for about 44 million American adults. Jogging one to five miles is part of the weekly routine for about six million Americans. People who are inactive are more likely to develop circulatory disorders, says modern medical science. Americans are taking these warnings seriously and investing more time and money in athletics. The investment is paying off by helping individuals of all ages feel better and stay healthier.

EXERCISES

Comprehension. Choose the correct answer.

1. The fastest growing sport in the United States is
   (a) ninepins.
   (b) fishing.
   (c) tennis.

2. A favorite outdoor sport of the middle-aged is
   (a) surfing.
   (b) golf.
   (c) football.

3. Three popular team sports in the United States are
   (a) bowling, fishing, and wrestling.
   (b) skiing, hunting, and chess.
   (c) baseball, football, and basketball.

4. A bat and ball are used in
   (a) bowling.
   (b) baseball.
   (c) golf.

5. In baseball, a point is called a
   (a) run.
   (b) strike.
   (c) home plate.

6. The most popular sporting event in the United States is the
   (a) American League.
   (b) home run.
   (c) World Series.

7. Football is played
   (a) on a flat field.
   (b) with a round ball.
   (c) with a ball and bat.

8. Basketball is played with
   (a) a large round ball.
   (b) protective helmets.
   (c) a ball and bat.

9. The object of basketball is to throw the ball into the opposing team's
   (a) end zone.
   (b) basket.
   (c) home plate.
10. Participation in sports is
   (a) on the rise.
   (b) decreasing.
   (c) remaining the same.

Vocabulary and Usage. Give the meaning of each of the following words. Use each in a sentence.

participation	spectator
athletics	amateur
equipment	competition
strenuous	attraction
professional	defensive

Conversation and Discussion. What is your favorite sport? How is it played?

XXII
Americans on Vacation

Since the 1940s, almost every American employee has received an annual vacation with pay, and it has become customary to use this time off for travel. The paid vacation varies in length, depending upon how long the employee has worked for his current employer. After a year's employment, two weeks' vacation is standard. After many years of service, a worker may get three or four weeks off. Those who are self-employed do not, of course, enjoy the "fringe benefit" of a paid vacation. But these people, too, customarily take vacations at least once a year.

Vacations are usually family affairs. Some families stay home to enjoy the local recreational facilities. But most vacationers prefer to travel, either within the United States or to other countries. Traveling within the United States is extremely popular because of a widespread desire to "see America first" and also because foreign travel generally requires more time and money. However, Americans who wish to vacation outside the country are free to go almost anywhere in the world. Obtaining a passport is a routine matter.

Our nation's major cities are among its most popular tourist attractions. *New York,* with a population of nearly 8 million, is the largest city in the United States and the second largest in the world. New York is located along the northern part of the East Coast at the mouth of the Hudson River. With a magnificent natural harbor and more than 500 miles of waterfront, it is the largest port in the world. The city is comprised of five sections called *boroughs*. The most important section is Manhattan, the commercial, cultural, and financial heart of the city. Manhattan is an island connected to the other boroughs by numerous bridges, tunnels, and ferries. The other boroughs are Brooklyn, the Bronx, Queens, and Richmond (most of which is Staten Island).

All year round, tourists jam the streets and hotels of Manhattan. They come to see the skyscrapers, particularly the gigantic Empire State Building (102 stories high), once the tallest building in the world and still among the tallest. They visit museums and art galleries, shop in enormous department stores and famous specialty shops, and eat in elegant and exotic restaurants. Other tourist attractions are the United Nations building, the New York Stock Exchange, and the Metropolitan Opera. This famous opera company now performs in the Lincoln Center for the Performing Arts, a complex of buildings constructed in the 1960s and containing, in addition to the opera house, theaters, a drama school, a music school, and a library-museum.

New York City is by far the nation's largest and finest area for theater. Within Manhattan, there are generally more than 40 different plays running simultaneously and about 200 different productions offered every year. New York theater falls into two categories—Broadway and off-Broadway. Broadway theaters are those in midtown Manhattan within a rectangle roughly ten blocks long and five blocks wide, surrounding part of the famous avenue called Broadway. These theaters offer a wide range of entertainment including musicals, comedies, and dramas. Generally, "big-name" people are involved—famous playwrights, important producers, nationally known performers. Settings are often lavish and ingenious, but most of the plays are conventional. Tickets are expensive and hard to get on short notice unless they are purchased from ticket agencies at more than box office prices.

Off-Broadway theater is quite different.The name does not refer to a specific geographical area but simply to plays performed in Manhattan outside the Broadway district. In these theaters, younger or unknown authors, producers, actors, and actresses learn their trade. The theaters are usually smaller, the seats less comfortable, the tickets much cheaper. Here the theatergoer will often find new plays, new faces onstage, and sometimes exciting, experimental productions.

New York is the landing point for visitors from many other countries. Approaching the city by ship, newcomers are greeted by the gigantic Statue of Liberty—symbol of freedom and opportunity.

Chicago is the second largest city in the nation and the largest city in the Midwest. To residents of surrounding areas, it offers the same attractions as New York, but on a smaller scale. Midwesterners come to Chicago to visit the theaters, restaurants, fine museums, and wide variety of stores. The elegant shops along Michigan Avenue and the huge department stores on State Street are particularly famous. Chicago is located on the shore of Lake Michigan. The city's Outer Drive Expressway along the lake gives travelers a scenic view of the beaches, harbors, parks, and skyscrapers, including the Sears, Roebuck building, the tallest in the world.

Chicago's favorite tourist attractions include the unique Museum of Science and Industry, which contains exhibits and elaborate working models showing applications of science to industry; Buckingham Fountain, the world's largest illuminated fountain; and the famous Art Institute. Visitors also like to walk through Old Town and New Town and browse in the many novelty shops.

Chicagoans boast of three major pieces of outdoor public art. On display in the downtown area is a fifty-foot sculptured head of a woman designed by Pablo Picasso. A few blocks away there will soon be another huge piece of sculpture (this one by Alexander Calder) and a gigantic mosaic (seventy feet long) designed by Marc Chagall.

Because of its central location, good transportation facilities, many hotels, and huge meeting places, Chicago is a popular choice for conventions—business, professional, and political.

The third largest city in the nation is *Los Angeles*, California. Hollywood, home of the American movie industry, is in L.A., and Disneyland, the nation's most fabulous amusement park, is nearby. Children, for whom Disneyland was built, are often taken there by curious parents, since it is a fascinating place for people of all ages.

Visitors to the West Coast often stop to see *San Francisco*. Situated between the Pacific Ocean and San Francisco Bay, the city is the leading seaport of the Pacific Coast. Ships come and go beneath its beautiful Golden Gate Bridge. Cable cars clang loudly as they climb the city's steep hills. San Francisco is famous for its bridges, cable cars, and breathtaking scenery. But tourists also come to enjoy fine dining—seafood on Fisherman's Wharf and Oriental cuisine in Chinatown.

Another great port city with exotic appeal for tourists is *New Orleans*, Louisiana. Located on the Mississippi River near the Gulf of Mexico, it contains many reminders of Old Europe and the Old South. The famous French Quarter, the Mardi Gras festival, and the Creoles (French-speaking descendants of early European settlers) all give the city a continental flavor. New Orleans is also the birthplace of jazz, and many people visit the city to hear good "Dixieland" music.

Vacationers interested in early American history and American government find the eastern part of the country fascinating. In *Washington, D.C.*, the nation's capital, visitors can watch Congress in action, attend a session of the Supreme Court, and tour the White House, the official home of the President. The Smithsonian Institution, with its six national museums, offers much of historical interest, including the Wright brothers' first airplane and a fine art collection. In Washington, there are also magnificent monuments honoring great statesmen, the most spectacular being the memorials to Washington, Lincoln, and Jefferson. *Philadelphia,* Pennsylvania is another famous historical city. It proudly displays the Liberty Bell, which rang to announce the signing of the Declaration of Independence in 1776. Visitors can also see the building where the United States Constitution was signed in 1787 and the home of Betsy Ross, who made the first American flag. Only 300 miles northeast of Philadelphia is *Boston,* Massachusetts, a city with many colonial landmarks and some of our nation's first and finest universities.

Whether visiting the East or the West, American vacationers often travel by automobile. About four out of every five American families own an automobile, and those that do not can rent one. For families, the automobile is probably the most economical way to travel. Many of them tour the nation by auto, driving from, for example, the Midwest to the West Coast, stopping to sightsee for part of the day and staying overnight at motels along the highways. Excellent interstate highways connect the nation's major cities. They enable vacationers to travel safely at almost a steady speed of fifty-five miles per hour.

American cities offer much for tourists to see. But since about 75 percent of Americans live in urban areas, many prefer to vacation in a rustic setting. For these people particularly, an automobile vastly increases recreational possibilities.

Camping has become extremely popular in recent years as conditions have become less primitive. Tiny house-type trailers can be hitched to the back of the family car for a relatively inexpensive mobile vacation. Some larger families have even converted old school buses into roomy campers. Many conveniently located camping sites make this economical form of family travel accessible to all.

Cars towing boats are a common sight on highways during the spring and summer months. Boating industry sources estimate that Americans own and use over 8 million pleasure boats. The popularity of boating has grown rapidly in the last twenty years as boats have become less expensive and more portable. A relatively new form of vacationing—houseboating—has also become popular. Since few families can afford to spend $10,000 to $50,000 to buy one of these floating cottages, rental facilities have sprung up along the nation's waterways, especially the Mississippi River.

In many parts of the country, cottages are rented during the summer months. City families find the cottage near the ocean or in the woods a refreshing change from urban life. Frequently, Mother and the children stay at the cottage all summer, and Dad drives up to spend weekends with the family.

For travelers interested in beautiful scenery, natural wonders, and wildlife, the United States has thirty-eight national parks in twenty-three states, covering more than 15 million acres. These parks are supervised by the U.S. National Park Service, which protects and preserves them. The largest national park, Yellowstone, encompasses about 3,500 square miles in Wyoming, Montana, and Idaho. Yellowstone contains the world's greatest geyser area, as well as spectacular waterfalls. The Grand Canyon in Arizona, Glacier National Park in Montana, and Yosemite in California are other popular western sites. In the East, there is the Florida Everglades, which makes up one of the largest swamplands in the world. This area is rich in bird and animal life. In addition to scenic spots, the National Park Service maintains many areas of historical and military interest. Every year more than 200 million visits are made to areas under National Park Service jurisdiction.

Throughout the nation there are resorts catering to all kinds of sports enthusiasts, as well as to vacationers who want just a rest and a suntan. There are dude ranches in the West, ski areas in many midwestern, northeastern, and western states, elegant hotel complexes in the mountains of New York, and resorts offering all sorts of water sports along the coasts and on many of the nation's lakes. Particularly beautiful and popular are the beaches of Hawaii and southern Florida, where visitors can swim and sunbathe the year round.

Summer vacations have become traditional because most children are not in school during July and August. However, many families take short winter vacations, too—especially during the Christmas season. Skiing, skating, snowmobiling, and various kinds of sledding are available in almost all the northern states during the winter months.

Because of this nation's great diversity of climate and geography, one can easily spend a lifetime of interesting vacations within the United States. Mountains, deserts, tropical regions, forests, oceans—all are here. Nevertheless, most Americans have an urge to visit other countries. Millions of Americans travel to Canada and Mexico every year. The islands of the Caribbean—Jamaica, Haiti, the Dominican Republic, and Puerto Rico—are also big tourist attractions. About 3 million Americans visit Europe every year. Airplanes have shortened the trip abroad from several days to several hours. Special group rates have lowered costs considerably. In addition, many airlines offer a "fly now, pay later" credit plan. All these factors have put long-distance travel within the reach of the average American, and many are taking advantage of the opportunity.

Whether traveling within the U.S.A. or abroad, for most

Americans a vacation provides a welcome opportunity for fun, relaxation, and a change of scene. It's a chance for family members to spend leisure time together and get to know each other better. The annual vacation is one of the happiest of American traditions.

EXERCISES

Comprehension. Choose the correct answer.

1. Most Americans spend their vacations in
   (a) Canada.
   (b) Europe.
   (c) the United States.
2. Most American workers receive an annual vacation
   (a) with pay.
   (b) without pay.
   (c) in Europe.
3. The United Nations is located in
   (a) Chicago.
   (b) New York.
   (c) Los Angeles.
4. Chicago is located on the shore of
   (a) Lake Erie.
   (b) Lake Huron.
   (c) Lake Michigan.
5. The Liberty Bell is on display in
   (a) Washington.
   (b) Philadelphia.
   (c) New York.
6. The Mardi Gras festival takes place in
   (a) Boston.
   (b) San Francisco.
   (c) New Orleans.

7. The United States Constitution was signed in
   (a) Boston.
   (b) Washington.
   (c) Philadelphia.

8. The most economical way for a family to travel in the United States is usually by
   (a) train.
   (b) automobile.
   (c) airplane.

9. Automobiles are owned by about
   (a) four out of five families.
   (b) three out of five families.
   (c) all families.

10. Each year, Europe is visited by about
    (a) 3 million Americans.
    (b) 2 million Americans.
    (c) 4 million Americans.

Vocabulary and Usage. Give the meaning of each of the following words. Use each in a sentence.

customary	require
specialty	surround
scenic	magnificent
landmark	rent
frequent	cater

Conversation and Discussion. Imagine that you are going to spend a vacation in the United States. Where will you go? What will you do?

XXIII
A Nation of Immigrants

In 1958, a young senator from Massachusetts published a book called *A Nation of Immigrants*. He was a wealthy and prominent American whose great-grandfather had come to the United States as a poor Irish immigrant. The author's name was John F. Kennedy.

In his book, President Kennedy pointed out, "Every American who ever lived . . . was either an immigrant himself or a descendant of immigrants." Even the American Indians were originally immigrants—descendants of Mongoloid peoples who came to the Western Hemisphere from Asia. The history of the United States is really the story of various immigrant groups working together to build a unique nation.

During the 1500s, French and Spanish explorers visited the New World. But the first Europeans who came to stay were mostly English. In 1607, 104 colonists established a community in Jamestown, Virginia. In 1620, 102 Pilgrims founded Plymouth Colony in Massachusetts. These were the modest beginnings of a nation that grew to 212 million in less than 400 years.

In 1790, when the first United States census was taken, the white population of the thirteen original states totaled slightly more than 3 million. About 75 percent of these first Americans were of British ancestry; the rest were German, Dutch, French, Swiss, and Spanish. The English gave the new nation its language, its laws, and its philosophy of government.

From 1820 to 1971, more than 45 million additional immigrants arrived—35.6 million from Europe, 1.7 million from Asia, 7.6 million from the Americas. This influx of people represented the largest migration that mankind has ever known. They came from everywhere, bringing with them the skills, ambition, and courage to convert a vast wilderness into a great industrial nation. The natural resources were here. But without workers who knew how to develop these resources, this country would have remained unsettled and untamed.

What made 45 million people leave their homelands to

come to a strange country? Said President Kennedy: "Three strong forces—religious persecution, political oppression, and economic hardship—provided the chief motives for the mass migrations to our shores."

American independence did not immediately stimulate immigration. Between 1790 and 1840, fewer than a million foreigners entered the country. But between 1841 and 1860, more than 4 million arrived. They came primarily from Ireland, Germany, Great Britain, and France and were driven here by poor harvests or political unrest. Potato crop failures in Ireland during the late 1840s stimulated Irish immigration. Germans came in great numbers because of economic and political difficulties. During the last half of the nineteenth century, many Scandinavians came, attracted by the abundance of good farmland. The Industrial Revolution and the Westward Movement gave new immigrants a vital role in the nation's economic development. Employers who needed factory workers and landowners who wanted tenants for western lands sent agents to Europe to "sell" America. Agents of steamship lines and railroad companies attracted thousands of immigrants with fabulous stories about "the land of opportunity."

Immigration took a tremendous leap after 1880. Between 1881 and 1920, 23.5 million aliens were admitted. Nearly 90 percent of these newcomers were from Europe. The government kept Asian immigration to a minimum after 1882 because American labor unions opposed the entry of immigrants from the Orient, fearing that they would threaten the jobs and depress the wage levels of white workers. In the 1890s the sources of European immigration began to shift. Between 1881 and 1890, 80 percent of American immigrants had come from northern and western Europe. By 1911, 77 percent were coming from southern and eastern Europe—Italy, Russia,

Austria-Hungary, Rumania, Bulgaria, Greece, and what were later to become Poland and Czechoslovakia. Many of those from Russia, Rumania, and Poland were Jews fleeing religious persecution.

During World War I, immigration declined due to traveling difficulties. After the war, Europeans once again began crowding aboard ships to the United States. But American industry no longer needed them. In 1921, Congress passed a quota law, limiting the number of Eastern Hemisphere immigrants for the first time. The limit was 350,000 annually. Subsequent laws reduced the annual quota even further.

From 1930 to 1945, legal limits and World War II kept immigration at a minimum. But after the war, immigration rose sharply because millions were left homeless by the war. About 4 million immigrants came to the United States between 1945 and 1964. Special legislation admitted large numbers of war brides, displaced persons, refugees, and orphans. In the late 1950s and early 1960s the United States relaxed quotas to allow thousands of Hungarians and more than 150,000 Cubans to enter the country. To relieve crowded conditions in Hong Kong, several thousand non-quota Chinese were also permitted entry.

The American population probably includes representatives of every existing nation. However, certain nationalities have dominated the immigration rolls. Since 1820, when the government first began keeping statistics on the national origins of immigrants, each of the following nations has sent 3 or more million people: Germany, Italy, Great Britain, Ireland, Austria-Hungary, Canada, and Russia.

Since most immigrants came from Europe, the racial makeup of the nation is about 88 percent Caucasian, 11 percent Negro, and 1 percent Mongoloid (including Chinese, Japanese, Polynesians, Eskimos, and American Indians).

In the twentieth century, the United States population has grown at a fantastic rate. In 1915, the population reached 100 million. Forty-two years later, it had doubled. Census experts predict that by the year 2000, there will be between 240 and 300 million Americans. A high birth rate, low infant mortality, and longer life expectancy have all helped to cause this "population explosion." Because of concern that the country may become overcrowded, efforts are being made to encourage various means of birth control.

Our soaring population has also forced the United States to maintain strict limits on immigration. In July, 1968, a new immigration law went into effect. Under this new law, there is an annual ceiling of 170,000 immigrant visas available to persons from the Eastern Hemisphere, regardless of their country of birth; however, no more than 20,000 can come from any one country. For natives of Western Hemisphere countries, 120,000 visas are available annually. In both categories, preference is given to relatives of American citizens or individuals with professions or skills needed in the United States.

In addition to those coming into the country as "quota immigrants," about 100,000 per year enter as "special immigrants" not counted in the numerical ceilings. These include immediate relatives of United States citizens, returning resident aliens, and a few other specified categories.

Who are today's immigrants? Of the 395,000 who entered the United States in 1972, about 90,000 came from Europe, 121,000 from Asia, and 151,000 from the Americas. The largest numbers of European immigrants are now coming from Italy, Greece, and Great Britain. Among Asian nations, the largest numbers come from the Philippines, Korea, and India. Western Hemisphere nations sending the most immigrants to the United States are Mexico, Canada, Cuba, and the West Indies.

The largest immigrant group in the United States today is the Spanish-speaking (Hispanic) group. Nearly 5 percent of Americans (about 10 million people) name Spanish as their mother tongue. Hispanic Americans form the second largest cultural minority in the United States, the largest being 23 million blacks. Nearly every state has residents representing the three major Hispanic groups—Mexican, Puerto Rican, and Cuban.

Mexican-Americans (Chicanos), numbering about 5 million, are the largest of the Hispanic groups. About 80 percent live in the Southwest, most of them in Texas and California. Los Angeles alone has a Mexican-American population of about 700,000. New Mexico, Arizona, and Colorado also have substantial Chicano populations.

Mexicans have an important place in American history. They helped to establish Los Angeles and many other settlements that later became major American cities. Also, they taught important methods of farming, mining, and ranching to Americans who settled in the West.

In the early 1600s, before the English came here, Spanish settlements sprang up in what is now New Mexico. In the 1700s, Mexican settlements moved north to California. When the Mexican-American War ended in 1848, the peace treaty gave the United States more than 525,000 square miles of territory in the Southwest, for which Mexico was paid $15 million. Mexicans living in this area were automatically granted American citizenship. No programs were created to Americanize these people, and the result was the development of a substantial Spanish-speaking population that remained linguistically and culturally unassimilated. Because of these Mexican-Americans, California, New Mexico, and Colorado all entered the union as bilingual states with state constitutional provisions requiring that all laws be published in Spanish as well as English.

Between 1910 and 1930, during the Mexican Revolution and a period of prosperity in the United States, nearly 2 million Mexicans immigrated here permanently. During this period, the term *Chicano* became a form of insult to Mexican-Americans. Today, it is the name Mexican-Americans use to refer proudly to themselves.

The Chicano movement, an aggressive attempt to improve the lot of Mexican-Americans, has been in the public eye since about 1965, when Cesar Chavez began organizing the California grape workers. He urged the public not to buy grapes and lettuce until the laborers who picked these products received decent wages, and his boycotts won nationwide support. Among the many aims of the Chicano movement are the following: to improve the political and economic status of Mexican-Americans; to encourage Chicanos to take pride in their Mexican heritage; to stimulate their interest in formal education; and to promote the literary use of the Mexican-American "language" called *Pocho*, a blend of Spanish, English, and some unique elements.

Leaders of the Chicano movement represent many different approaches and goals. Some are advocates of nonviolence. Others are militants, separatists, or nationalists. Some feel that political power is the most direct route to social and economic improvement.

Whatever the solution, there is no doubt that the life of the Mexican-American needs to be improved. Their education, income, employment, housing, and health are all significantly below national averages. The migrant farm workers especially have a hard life. In 1967, their average life expectancy was only forty-nine years!

Puerto Ricans (numbering about 1.4 million in 1971) are the second largest Hispanic group in the United States. Nearly 70 percent live in or near New York City. Many hold important positions there in business, education, government, and the arts. Dozens of Puerto Rican writers, actors, and entertainers have made valuable contributions to American culture, including screen star José Ferrer, blind guitarist José Feliciano, and baseball player Roberto Clemente. Ceded to the United States by Spain in 1898, Puerto Rico is a free commonwealth with its own government. All Puerto Ricans are United States citizens.

Cuban immigrants and their children make up the third largest group of Spanish-Americans. More than 600,000 Cubans are now living in the United States. Most of them came here as exiles during or after 1959, when Fidel Castro took over the Cuban government. About 40 percent live in Florida, primarily in the Miami area. The Cuban Refugee Center in Miami has provided assistance to those who wished to resettle in other parts of the country. Federal financial aid has been available to those who have needed it. Cubans who came to the United States after 1958, can, after living in this country for two years, obtain permanent resident status.

This nation of immigrants is rapidly becoming a nation of native-born citizens. Today, the number of foreign-born in the United States makes up only about 4 percent of the population, and only 11 percent of Americans are the children of immigrants. The days of mass immigration are probably behind us. But the influence of the movement will never be erased. Americans have adopted many of the customs and ideas of the immigrants as their own. President Kennedy explained it this way: ". . . each wave of immigration left its own impact on American society; each made its distinctive 'contribution' to the building of the nation and the evolution of American life."

The wide variety of immigrant groups in the United States has given the nation great industrial diversity. Germans, Scandinavians, and Poles share the credit for turning millions of acres of wilderness into productive farmland. Scandinavians also helped to develop the lumbering industry, along with Canadians. The Swedes built the first log cabins. The Swiss brought clock-making and cheese-making skills. The English were experienced in the handling of horses, cattle, and sheep. The Greeks, Italians, Portuguese, and Spanish grew citrus fruits and grapes. Italians started our domestic wine industry. Chinese and Irish laborers built the first railroad that spanned the nation.

In addition to their skills, immigrants brought their native customs and beliefs—political and social theories, religions, academic traditions, holidays, festivals, sports, arts, hobbies, foods—and by doing so, they greatly enriched American culture. The Germans introduced the Christmas tree, kindergarten, glee clubs, and the symphony orchestra. The Dutch brought the art of growing tulips, ice-skating, bowling, golf, and Santa Claus. The French taught Americans elegant continental cooking and dancing. Italians brought their talents in painting, sculpture, and architecture. The Irish firmly established the Catholic Church as an English-speaking institution (originally, on this continent, it was French), introduced parochial schools, and built many Catholic colleges. The Irish also became active in politics and organized the first big nationwide labor union.

The American diet has also been delightfully affected by various immigrant groups. The Dutch taught us to make waffles and doughnuts. The Germans brought hamburgers, sausages, sauerbraten, sauerkraut, and blintzes. Italians introduced Americans to pizza, spaghetti, minestrone, ravioli, and antipasto. Americans enjoy Swiss cheeses and fondue, Irish stew, Chinese egg rolls and chow mein, tacos, teriyaki, curries, caviar, gefilte fish, shish kebab, Yorkshire pudding, yogurt, Danish pastry, chocolate mousse, and Turkish coffee. These are just a few of the foreign foods which frequently appear on American dinner tables.

For immigrants from all parts of the world, the United States has been a "melting pot," in which they have become one people who share a common culture and a common loyalty. But when we say that the United States is a melting pot, we do not mean that it melts away all recollections of another way of life in another place. Most immigrants treasure all their lives the traditions of their homeland and share a special bond with people of the same national origin. Immigrants from the same "old country" tend to settle in the same neighborhoods and establish their native religious and social institutions. Immigrant parents often try to pass on to their children the language, culinary skills, religious customs, and moral outlook that are their heritage. Often there is conflict between the ideas of the "old country" and those of the new one. Nevertheless, despite the need for tremendous adjustments, most immigrants learn to love their adopted land. Some of the most patriotic Americans are those who have lived and suffered elsewhere. Undoubtedly, the United States owes its great prosperity and its strength to the fact that it is, in John Kennedy's words, a nation of immigrants.

EXERCISES

Comprehension. Choose the correct answer.

1. The first to immigrate to America were
   (a) the Spanish.
   (b) the ancestors of the American Indians.
   (c) the Pilgrims.
2. The first Europeans who came to stay were mostly
   (a) English.
   (b) French.
   (c) Spanish.
3. How many immigrants came to the U.S.A. between 1820 and 1971?
   (a) About 90 million.
   (b) About 45 million.
   (c) About 50 million.
4. Irish immigration in the 1840s was stimulated by
   (a) free passage.
   (b) potato crop failures.
   (c) great wealth.
5. Most immigrants to the United States were driven here by
   (a) idealism.
   (b) crop failures and political unrest.
   (c) a desire to visit their families.
6. The vast majority of immigrants to the U.S.A. came from
   (a) Europe.
   (b) Latin America.
   (c) Asia.
7. Asian immigration was limited by
   (a) the great distance.
   (b) war.
   (c) labor union opposition.

8. In the twentieth century, immigration has declined because of
   (a) war and quotas.
   (b) improved conditions.
   (c) European restrictions.

9. One custom which was introduced by immigrants is
   (a) baseball.
   (b) the Fourth of July.
   (c) the Christmas tree.

10. The number of foreign-born in the United States today is only about
    (a) 20 percent.
    (b) 4 percent.
    (c) 9 percent.

Vocabulary and Usage. Give the meaning of each of the following words. Use each in a sentence.

descendant	wilderness
census	stimulate
crowded	motive
soar	skill
conclude	persecute

Conversation and Discussion. Many immigrants to the United States have become very famous men. Name as many famous American immigrants as you can.

XXIV
The Black American

"If you're white, you're all right; . . . if you're black, git back, git back, git back" warn the lyrics of a well-known American song. But times are changing. Now, after years of degradation, the black American is stepping forward to demand the equality promised to him in the Constitution.

In the fifteenth century, Europeans began to import

slaves from the African continent. The discovery of the Americas increased the demand for cheap labor and therefore increased the slave trade. Slave traders from Europe and America tapped the human resources of Africa for about 400 years. In all, more than 15 million people are believed to have been carried from Africa by slave merchants. By the time the American Civil War began in 1860, there were about 4.5 million Negroes in the United States, most of them slaves.

Before the Civil War, the vast majority of Negro slaves lived in the South, where they worked in cotton, tobacco, and sugar cane fields. Most were uneducated, although a few were taught to read and write. Their African religious practices were discouraged, and they were converted to Christianity.

The slaves suffered greatly, both physically and emotionally. They worked long hours in the fields. They lived in crowded, primitive dwellings. Some were the victims of cruel masters who whipped them. Often, slaveowners separated Negro families by selling a slave's husband, wife, or child. *Uncle Tom's Cabin*, a famous novel about Southern slavery, emphasized these evils. The book aroused so much antislavery sentiment in the North that Abraham Lincoln once said to its author, Harriet Beecher Stowe, "So you're the little woman who wrote the book that made this great war."

In 1863, Lincoln's Emancipation Proclamation freed the slaves in the Confederate states. Shortly after the Civil War ended in 1865, the Thirteenth Amendment to the Constitution was adopted. This amendment freed all slaves. A few years later, the Fourteenth and Fifteenth Amendments declared that the former slaves were citizens entitled to full civil rights and equal suffrage. The Fifteenth Amendment says that an American citizen's voting privilege "shall not be denied or abridged by the United States or by any State on account of race, color, or previous condition of servitude."

By 1870, the black American had been declared a citizen with all the rights guaranteed to every citizen. But he was a member of a conspicuous minority group within a white society. Furthermore, he was uneducated, unskilled, and unprepared to provide for his own basic needs. With freedom, the Negro found many new problems —legal, social, and economic.

After the Civil War, Negroes began migrating north to the cities. Now about one-half of the nation's 23 million blacks live in the North or West, and three out of every five live in the central city of a major metropolitan area.

In the North, blacks found greater freedom than in the South, but discrimination by private citizens has made conditions difficult and opportunities limited. Discrimination in the sale and rental of housing forced blacks into densely populated, segregated communities often referred to as ghettos. (New York City's Harlem is the best known of these areas.) This segregated housing pattern created segregated schools because students have traditionally been assigned to schools in their neighborhoods. For a variety of reasons, schools in black communities are generally academically behind schools in white areas, and black children are less likely than white children to finish high school or enter college. With less education, they are poorly equipped to compete in the job market. This fact, coupled with discrimination in hiring, has caused the unemployment rate among blacks to be about double the figure for whites. The high unemployment rate is a factor causing higher crime rates among blacks, which in turn heightens prejudice against them.

Blacks who remained in the South endured conditions even more difficult and degrading. Southern blacks were forced to obey state laws (called *Jim Crow laws*) which kept them segregated from white people. The races went to different schools, drank from different fountains, used different washrooms, ate in different restaurants, and were buried in different cemeteries. On buses, blacks were required to sit in the back. For the Southern black, there was no such thing as justice in the courts of law. Once he was accused of a crime, it was probable that a white jury would find him guilty.

Southern whites, who wished to keep the power of the vote from the large black population of the South, used the threat of violence to discourage blacks from registering to vote. When a black person did try to register, devices such as a poll tax (a tax on the right to vote) or a literacy test (unfairly administered) were used to deny him his right.

The first break in the South's rigidly segregated way of life came in 1954 when the U.S. Supreme Court declared that no state could separate schoolchildren by race. Thereafter, many other discriminatory practices were declared illegal, but only after long and expensive court battles which usually were decided by the U.S. Supreme Court.

The Supreme Court's school desegregation decision stimulated black hopes for a better life in the United States. During the mid-1950s, blacks throughout the nation began demanding equal rights. Their "revolution" started as a nonviolent movement consisting of boycotts, "sit-ins" (blacks calmly sitting for hours at lunch counters or in restaurants that refused to serve them), "freedom rides" (busloads of Northern liberals coming to the South to force integration of public facilities), and protest marches. But during the 1960s, the struggle led to violence, committed by both blacks and whites. Angry, militant blacks preached armed rebellion. Many cities were disturbed by riots which involved burglary, arson, and street battles between rioters and police. In several cities, national guard units had to assist local police in quelling disturbances.

Perhaps these incidents alarmed the white population into doing more to help black people. In 1964, the 24th Amendment to the Constitution was adopted; it prohibited poll taxes in federal elections. From 1957 to 1970, six major civil rights bills were passed by Congress. Some of these laws protected black voting rights by outlawing literacy tests, authorizing the appointment of federal examiners to register voters in areas of marked discrimination, and providing stiff penalties for those who interfere with voting rights. As a result, the nation gained 2 million new black voters, and hundreds of Southern blacks were elected to public office.

Also during the 1960s, blacks began receiving more federal, state, and local help in satisfying their most urgent needs: to obtain better jobs and decent places to live. Urban renewal projects tore down many slum buildings and replaced them with low-cost, high-rise buildings. Some low-cost public housing was built in neighborhoods that were, until then, all white. Many industries which once refused to employ blacks began seeking them out. Government training programs and federal funds helped the unskilled learn trades. Between 1960 and 1970, total employment of blacks increased 22 percent while their employment in professional, technical, and clerical occupations doubled. About 13 percent of black workers now hold professional or managerial positions, and the number of black-owned businesses is growing rapidly. Still, about two-fifths of blacks are employed as household help, laborers, and agricultural workers, a much greater proportion than whites in these menial jobs.

Clearly, during the 1960s blacks made great gains in education. By 1970, the illiteracy rate among black adolescents and young adults was less than one percent, compared with nine percent of the older population. Also by 1970, 56 percent of all young black adults had completed high school, compared with 38 percent in 1960. By 1973, nearly one-half of black high school graduates were enrolling in college.

Also during the 1960s, there were continued efforts to make school desegregation a reality. The U.S. Supreme Court applied pressure to Southerners who were trying to circumvent the school desegregation order. The Court demanded that public schools be desegregated at once. In several Northern cities, some black students were bused to schools in white communities. Still, in 1971, 61 percent of black students attended schools that were nearly all black, and 65 percent of white students attended schools that were nearly all white.

Race relations during the 1960s changed considerably as black Americans developed greater self-esteem. No longer would they accept the white man's judgment that to be black is to be inferior. The popular slogan "black is beautiful" emphatically expressed the black man's new pride in himself. The American of African descent rejected the name *Negro* and now refers to himself as Afro-American or, more commonly, as black. For some blacks, the new terminology was accompanied by a growing sense of identification with their African heritage. As a result, African hairdos and African styles of dress became fashionable among blacks. Courses in black history became commonplace in school curriculums as blacks became interested in studying about their African heritage and their part in the development of the United States. Many demanded a rewriting of textbooks to give students a true picture of the important role of blacks in the nation's history.

In 1952, a black writer, Ralph Ellison, wrote a book about the black situation in the United States and entitled it *The Invisible Man*. In the 1960s, Ellison's invisible man became visible. Suddenly, TV advertisers began using some black models in their commercials. Suddenly, a new type of TV show developed—talk shows for blacks, dealing essentially with the interests of the black community. More urban newspapers began supplying magazine supplements directed to black readers. Suddenly, news media and advertisers responded to the fact that 11 percent of Americans are black and that they, too, are consumers.

The 1970s brought a decline in public concern about black needs. The Administration and the general public turned their attention to other problems. To save money, federal funds for many programs that helped the ghetto blacks have been cut back. Busing only for the purpose of achieving integration has been outlawed. Most of the prominent black leaders of the 1960s are gone now, and the new leaders disagree as to methods and goals of black advancement. The black "revolution" seems past its prime, and progress has slowed down. But the giant steps forward taken during the 1960s changed the black American into a new person with a healthier self-image, a greater number of opportunities, and a good chance to continue to advance, though perhaps at a slower pace.

Although blacks made great advancements during the 1960s, their fight for equality continues. Enforcement of the civil rights laws is still grossly inadequate. Discrimination still prevents blacks from participating fully in American society. Blacks and other minorities still control less than 4 percent of American business. Median family income for black families is about $6,800 compared to about $11,500 for white families. A shocking 43 percent of black children are growing up in poverty, compared to 15 percent of white youngsters.

Life in the black ghettos of the cities is frightful and frightening. Neighborhoods are in depressingly poor condition, with deteriorated buildings, abandoned tenements, burned-out businesses, and empty lots containing nothing but weeds and broken glass. The crime rate is high, the problem of drug addiction is immense, and the fear of warring youth gangs makes residents hesitate to go out after dark.

Black leaders of the 1970s are exerting most of their efforts toward increasing two kinds of black power —economic and political. Despite some economic setbacks, during the '70s federal hiring of blacks has been expanded and federal aid to minority businesses and colleges has vastly increased.

In politics, black gains have been phenomenal. The black vote in the eleven states of the Old South seated more than 1,000 black officials in 1973, compared to fewer than 100 before 1965. In the North, about 1,500 blacks held elective office in 1973. The 93rd Congress contained 17 blacks, 16 in the House and one in the Senate. (In 1967, Edward Brooke of Massachusetts became the first black elected to the Senate in about 100 years.)

Despite present and past deprivations, black Americans have made important contributions to the United States. The chief influence of the American Negro culture —nationally and internationally—has been in the field of music. The familiar Negro spirituals, the unusual rhythms and harmonies of jazz, the haunting "blues" melodies—all these originated with the Negro slaves. It is often said that what is best and most original in American popular music is that which derives its style from the Negro idiom. The music of Stephen Foster, George Gershwin, and W. C. Handy are well-known examples.

The list of contributions made by individual blacks is endless. Many are highly respected professional people —teachers, doctors, lawyers, judges, and ministers. Many have attained nationwide and worldwide fame as great authors, athletes, entertainers, musicians, scientists, and statesmen. In 1967, Thurgood Marshall became the first black ever appointed as a justice of the U.S. Supreme Court. Two black Americans have won the Nobel Peace Prize. In 1950, Ralph Bunche, a United Nations mediator, won the award for his success in negotiating an armistice between Israel and the Arab League. In 1964, Martin Luther King, Jr. won the peace prize for his leadership of black America's nonviolent protest. Since his assassination in 1968, King has become a national hero. In many cities, his birthday is a holiday.

Given an equal opportunity to learn and to work, the black American will be able to contribute even more to his country. In order to make full use of its human resources, the United States must be sure that its customs and institutions extend equal privileges to all American citizens.

EXERCISES

Comprehension. Choose the correct answer.

1. The ancestors of black Americans were brought to the United States as
   (a) serfs.
   (b) slaves.
   (c) immigrants.

2. Before the Civil War, most slaves lived in the
   (a) North.
   (b) South.
   (c) West.

3. *Uncle Tom's Cabin* was written by
   (a) Betsy Ross.
   (b) Lincoln.
   (c) Harriet Beecher Stowe.

4. All slaves were finally freed by the
   (a) Emancipation Proclamation.
   (b) Thirteenth Amendment.
   (c) Dred Scott decision.

5. In the southern United States, Negroes have been
   (a) reasonably well-treated.
   (b) continually oppressed.
   (c) happy and content.

6. A major advance in the civil rights struggle came with
   (a) the 1954 Supreme Court decision on school desegregation.
   (b) the Nobel Peace Prize.
   (c) migration to the North.

7. Since the Civil War, blacks have been migrating north to the
   (a) farms.
   (b) cities.
   (c) suburbs.

8. The black population in the United States is now about
   (a) 2.3 million.
   (b) 12 million.
   (c) 23 million.

9. The Negro unemployment rate is
   (a) lower than that of the white population.
   (b) the same as the white population's.
   (c) higher than that of the white population.

10. One great Negro contribution to the culture of the United States and the world has been in the field of
    (a) philosophy.
    (b) music.
    (c) painting.

Vocabulary and Usage. Give the meaning of each of the following words. Use each in a sentence.

conspicuous	integration
segregate	discriminate
boycott	ghetto
militant	distrust
privilege	assassination

Conversation and Discussion. Discuss some of the contributions that blacks have made to American life.

XXV
The American Indian

The people we now call *American Indians* came to the Western Hemisphere from Asia more than 20,000 years ago. Most of them settled in the warm, fertile plains of Mexico, Central America, and South America. By the fifteenth century there were 15 to 20 million Indians in the Americas. Perhaps as many as 700,000 were living within the present limits of the United States when Columbus discovered the New World in 1492. It was Columbus who first called these people *Indians* because he thought he had reached the East Indies when he landed in San Salvador.

President Kennedy once called American Indians "the least understood and most misunderstood Americans of us all." Legends of the "Wild West" have often distorted the role of the Indian in the development of America. The American Indian is frequently depicted as a cruel and ignorant savage. True, some tribes did react violently to the European invasion of their land, but that is only half of the story. When white men first arrived in North America, most Indians were friendly and eager to teach the newcomers how to get along in a strange land. For example, without Indian assistance, the Pilgrims in Massachusetts might not have survived.

The most famous Indian friend of the white settlers was a young princess named Pocahontas. She was only twelve years old when English settlers came to Jamestown, Virginia in 1607. In 1608, Captain John Smith, one of these early colonists, wrote that he owed his life to Pocahontas, who threw her arms around Smith to prevent her father, the chief, from harming him. After that, she was a frequent visitor to the English fort and often brought gifts of food and other necessities. Despite her many kindnesses to the settlers, at the age of seventeen she was kidnapped by them to guarantee the good behavior of her tribe. The following year, Pocahontas married one of the colonists and later traveled with him to England, where she was introduced to high society and became an object of great curiosity. While in London, she died of smallpox at the age of twenty-one, leaving a son from whom many prominent Virginians claim descent. Her life story has been the subject of several fictional works and is well known to most Americans.

Of all the Indians' gifts to the settlers, food was probably the most valuable. Indian foods and Indian methods of planting, hunting, and fishing enabled settlers to survive in their strange new home. Two of the most important crops in the world—corn and white potatoes—were first domesticated by American Indians, who also introduced the settlers to more than eighty other foods, including the sweet potato, pumpkin, squash, peanut, tomato, banana, pineapple, and avocado.

The Indians showed the settlers how to cook these unfamiliar plants to make grits, hominy, popcorn, succotash, and tapioca. Cacao (for chocolate), chicle (for chewing gum), and tobacco were also among Indian crops. Many of the drugs which Indians extracted from plants are still being used today, such as cocaine, a pain reliever obtained from coca.

"Redskins" also helped the settlers by introducing them to Indian utensils, clothing, trails, and methods of transportation. Indian inventions adopted by American settlers included hammocks, canoes, dog sleds, toboggans, pipes, rubber balls, snowshoes, moccasins, parkas, and ponchos.

The influence of Indian cultures upon the European settlers is evident in American English. In the Western Hemisphere, thousands of mountains, lakes, rivers, cities, states, and countries have Indian names—Chicago, Massachusetts, Oregon, Mexico, Nicaragua, and Peru, to mention just a few. Indian words in the English language include skunk, moose, tobacco, succotash, squash, and hundreds of others.

Indian assistance to the European settlers was immeasurable. Only when the white man began pushing the Indian off his land did the Indian view him as an enemy to be vanquished. Most settlers who came to the colonies wanted Indian territories. The British and Americans made hundreds of treaties with various Indian tribes, paying for large areas of land with cash or merchandise. But the white men cheated the Indians and violated most of these treaties. As a result, there were many small but bloody wars. The Indians were doomed to defeat. The settlers had guns; the Indians fought mostly with bows and arrows. The settlers were able to unite against their common enemy, whereas the Indians were divided into hundreds of separate tribes which were hostile to each other. Having no understanding or appreciation of Indian culture, the settlers considered the Indian an inferior savage and felt no qualms about dispossessing him. They did so as quickly and completely as possible.

As early as 1786, the United States government began setting aside special territories (reservations) for Indian resettlement. In 1830, Congress passed the Indian Removal Act, which forced Indians to move west of the Mississippi River to arid land which the white settlers considered undesirable. As the nineteenth century and the Westward Movement progressed, the Indians were forced onto smaller and smaller reservations. For many years they were confined to these reservations and forbidden to leave without a permit. Many of their religious and social customs were banned. Toward the end of the nineteenth century, government policies were mainly directed toward decreasing Indian territorial holdings and encouraging Indian assimilation into the white culture. As a result of poverty and poor living conditions, the Indians suffered greatly. By 1890, their population had dwindled to about 240,000.

In the 1920s, American attitudes and policies concerning Indians began to improve; as a result, the population grew. Today there are about 800,000 Indians living in the United States. All are American citizens and have the right to vote. Although they are free to live on or off reservations, the majority have remained on their reserved land.

Reservations are under the control of the federal government rather than the separate states in which they exist. The Bureau of Indian Affairs (BIA) counts 282 Indian reservations, plus about 150 other land units managed for Indians by the federal government. Most of these are owned by tribes, and the balance belongs to individual Indians. Units range in size from a few acres to the vast Navajo reservation, which covers 24,000 square miles in Arizona, New Mexico, and Utah. Altogether, more than 50 million acres are owned and occupied by Indians.

Most Indians live in the Southwest—Arizona, Oklahoma, New Mexico, and California. However, some tribes live in the Northwest—in North Dakota, South Dakota, Wyoming, and Montana. Alaska has an Indian population of about 35,000, including 16,000 Eskimos. Strung along the East Coast are dozens of small Indian communities.

On the reservations, traditional Indian customs, languages, and styles of dress have survived. Every year thousands of tourists visit these reservations to observe the Indian way of life and to witness Indian dances, games, races, and festivals.

Except for a few tribes lucky enough to have found natural resources such as oil on their property, most Indians are poor. They depend largely upon the land for sustenance, and often the land is not rich enough to support the tribe's population. Some reservations that do possess valuable natural resources lack funds to develop their underground wealth. Most reservation Indians earn a meager living from farming or raising livestock. Still others work on farms or in factories or mines near their reservations. A small percentage are professional people—teachers, nurses, and doctors.

In recent years, BIA efforts have introduced about 100 new industrial plants and commercial enterprises on reservations. But the well-established handmade crafts industry still employs about 5,000 Indians. Various tribes make baskets, pottery, woven blankets and rugs, wood sculpture, beadwork, and silver jewelry with turquoise stones. Most Indian products have attractive, colorful designs. Because of their beauty and fine, durable workmanship, these goods are purchased by tourists from all over the country.

Indians have a difficult time finding jobs off the reservation for several reasons: some know very little English; some are illiterate; and many live on reservations located in isolated areas where there is little or no opportunity for employment.

In search of greater prosperity, some Indians choose to leave the reservation and find jobs and homes in the cities. The federal government is eager to assist those who wish to assimilate, and every year increasing numbers of Indians try it. In 1960, only about 28 percent of Indians in the United States lived in cities. Today, with a larger Indian population, about 45 percent are urban dwellers. But many Indians have trouble adjusting to a highly competitive capitalistic and materialistic culture. Tribal attitudes and values are quite different from those of mainstream America. For example, Indians believe that the land and its produce cannot be the property of any individual but belong to the group. Then, as a prominent Indian artist explained, "Indians are not materialistic. They don't have to have *things* the way white society does." Moreover, what little Indians do have they are usually willing to share with relatives or friends who have less. Also, Indians are not competitive. "Success is unpopular," said one official on an Apache reservation. In school, for example, Indian children try to assist rather than outdo one another. Thus, some of the finest Indian virtues actually interfere with success in contemporary America.

On or off the reservation, American Indians are one of the most deprived and most unhappy of minority groups in this country. Their education, income, housing, and health are all far below national averages. Nearly 60 percent of Indians have less than an eighth grade education, and their high school dropout rate is almost double the national average. Unemployment runs about 40 percent, and on some reservations exceeds 75 percent. About four-fifths of reservation Indians have incomes below the poverty level. Most of them live in substandard housing —huts, shanties, even abandoned automobiles. Alcohol is a major problem for a large percentage of Indians. The high incidence of infectious diseases, malnutrition, infant mortality, and suicide makes Indian life expectancy about six years less than the national average.

The federal government is now spending about a billion dollars a year to help the Indians. Through the BIA, the government provides educational facilities and opportunities for economic development. The Bureau operates more than 200 schools in remote areas where state public schools are not available to Indian children. The BIA also provides opportunities for vocational training and higher education. Economic assistance has come in many forms. For example, federal funds have employed Indians in projects designed to improve reservations by road construction, forest preservation, soil and moisture conservation, development of natural resources, and construction of new recreational facilities.

In the past, most Americans were convinced that the way to help Indians was by teaching them English, converting them to Christianity, and getting them off the reservations and out into the mainstream of American life. But most Indians have resisted attempts to assimilate them, fearing that assimilation means annihilation. They do not want to see their cultures destroyed, not even for the sake of economic prosperity.

During the 1960s, a noticeable Indian activist movement began to develop. Under the direction of Indian leaders, there have been many highly publicized, dramatic "incidents" to remind white Americans of past and present injustices to Indians. Indians have demonstrated publicly, setting up tepees on city streets, taking over public buildings, stealing government documents, even holding hostages in order to call attention to their situation. They have also demanded (and in some cases received) repayment for lands taken from them by the government in violation of treaties. Most important, they have demanded an end to white paternalism.

The government has been quite responsive to Indian pressures for administrative control of their own property and services. In 1970, the President announced a new national policy concerning Indians, a policy that would encourage Indian control of Indian affairs but would not deprive Indians of government assistance when and where they needed it. An Indian is now the Commissioner of Indian Affairs. Tribal leaders are involved in making decisions about education, medical care, industrial development, conservation, and other federal programs on reservations. And government funding has established Navajo Community College, the first college located on an Indian reservation and operated by an Indian tribe.

White Americans are finally coming to realize that Indian tribes with separate identities and cultures are here to stay. But even more significant, many whites are beginning to appreciate the timeless wisdom of the Indian world. Our growing national concern about ecology helps us to understand the Indian reluctance to disturb the balance of nature. Our growing dissatisfaction with materialism leads us to a greater appreciation of the Indian outlook.

After two centuries of suffering, the American Indian may now find more opportunities for a good life in this land that was once his own, among people to whom he has given so much.

EXERCISES

Comprehension. Choose the correct answer.

1. The ancestors of the American Indian came from
   (a) Africa.
   (b) Asia.
   (c) Europe.
2. Columbus first called these people Indians because
   (a) he thought he had reached the East Indies.
   (b) that was the name they told him.
   (c) he read the name in a book.
3. When Europeans first came to America, the Indians were
   (a) friendly.
   (b) violent.
   (c) indifferent.
4. At first, the Indians fought with
   (a) guns.
   (b) bows and arrows.
   (c) stones.
5. Special territories established by the federal government for the Indians are called

(a) reservations.
(b) homesteads.
(c) settlement centers.

6. Many Indians were forced to move west of the Mississippi by the
(a) Bureau of Indian Affairs.
(b) Indian reservation.
(c) Indian Removal Act.

7. The present Indian population in the United States is about
(a) 100,000.
(b) 400,000.
(c) 800,000.

8. Indians receive financial aid from
(a) the Bureau of Indian Affairs.
(b) their own governments.
(c) the Indian Removal Act.

9. For most Indians, earning a living is
(a) easy.
(b) difficult.
(c) effortless.

10. The Indians introduced the colonial settlers to
(a) liquor.
(b) pumpkins and squash.
(c) carbonated beverages.

Vocabulary and Usage. Give the meaning of each of the following words. Use each in a sentence.

wigwam
territory
hammock
permit
assimilation
vanquished
treaty
appreciation
meager
soil

Conversation and Discussion. Have you ever visited an Indian reservation? Discuss some of the contributions which the Indians have made to American culture.

XXVI
The Constitution and the Federal System

THE CONSTITUTION

Daniel Webster, the eloquent nineteenth-century American statesman, once said: "We may be tossed upon an ocean where we can see no land—nor, perhaps, the sun or stars. But there is a chart and a compass for us to study, to consult, and to obey. That chart is the Constitution."

What is this Constitution? It is the basic law from which the United States government derives all its power. It is the law that protects the inhabitants of this nation from arbitrary actions by the federal government or any individual state.

The Constitution defines three distinct branches of our national government. They are the legislative branch, which enacts laws; the executive branch, which enforces them; and the judicial branch, which interprets them.

The legislative branch is called Congress. It is made up of two houses—the Senate and the House of Representatives. The Senate is often referred to as the "upper house" and is composed of two senators from each state. Senators are elected for six-year terms. Every two years, one-third of them face reelection.

The "lower house" is the House of Representatives, which consists of 435 members. The representation of each state is determined by the state's population. So, while the smallest states have only one representative each, California's representation in the 93rd Congress (1973-1974) was 43. The entire House is elected every two years.

For the purpose of electing representatives, each state is divided into Congressional districts. The districts within a state are approximately equal in population. One representative is elected from each district. One of his major obligations is protecting the interests of the people in his district.

The job of Congress is to make laws. Before a proposed law (bill) becomes enacted, it must be approved by both houses of Congress and by the President. The powers of Congress and its limitations are specified in the Constitution.

The President is the nation's chief executive. He must see that all national laws are carried out. Naturally, he has a large staff of advisers and other employees to assist him. The most important group of advisers is called the Cabinet. The Cabinet includes the heads of the eleven departments of the executive branch. They are chosen by the President with the advice and consent of the Senate. The President also appoints ambassadors and other consular heads, as well as judges of the federal courts.

The Vice-President is the only other elected person in the executive branch. His chief constitutional duty is to preside over the Senate. His most important function is to succeed to the presidency upon the death, resignation, or disability of the President. Out of thirty-two presidents elected, eight have died in office and one resigned. In each case, the Vice-President succeeded to the presidency.

The judicial branch is composed of the federal courts. They are the U.S. District Courts, where trials are conducted; the Courts of Appeals; and the U.S. Supreme Court.

One of the unusual features of the American judicial system is the power of the courts to declare legislation unconstitutional and, therefore, void. Federal laws are unconstitutional if they are in excess of Congress's authority, or if they would infringe upon individual rights protected by the Constitution. State laws are unconstitutional if they conflict with federal laws or with that state's constitution.

United States laws are in some way controlled or affected by all three branches of government—Congress enacts them; the President approves and enforces them; and the courts determine their validity and interpret them. This is one example of the government's system of "checks and balances," by which each branch prevents improper actions by the other branches.

The checks and balances were put to a severe test in 1974 when it was discovered that President Nixon had been involved in obstruction of justice in connection with the "Watergate" scandal. (See Chapter XXVII.) Both Congress and the special "Watergate" prosecutor demanded that the President turn over to them certain documents and tape recordings in his possession. The President said that, since the Constitution divided the government into three distinct branches, neither the judicial branch nor the legislative branch had any control over the executive branch (the President). This division is often referred to as the "separation of powers."

During this conflict between the President and the other two branches of government, some of the questions raised were: Could the President withhold information regarding himself and his aides from Congress and the courts? Did the doctrine of separation of powers prohibit the courts from ordering the President to submit evidence in his possession to the prosecutor's office? Or, conversely, did the President have the right to be the final interpreter of the Constitution? What conduct by a President was sufficient to justify his removal from office?

The outcome was that the Supreme Court reaffirmed itself as final interpreter of the Constitution and entered an order that the President submit the evidence to the prosecutor. Congress commenced the Constitutional procedure to remove the President from office (impeachment) and, ultimately, President Nixon resigned. The "checks and balances" prevented a major governmental crisis, and the presidency passed peacefully and smoothly to the Vice-President. The "chart" had kept the country on course, even when the captain tried to veer.

Probably the most significant and far-reaching portion of the Constitution is the Bill of Rights, comprising the first ten amendments to the Constitution. The first of these assures freedom of religion, speech, and the press and the right of peaceful assembly. Speech is protected no matter how unpopular or repulsive, so long as it does not create an immediate and serious danger to life or property. Free speech is at the very heart of democracy. As former Supreme Court Justice Brandeis once said: "In frank expression of conflicting opinion lies the greatest promise of wisdom in governmental action; and in suppression lies ordinarily the greatest peril."

Freedom of religion means that each person can belong to any church and follow its dictates, so long as these do not seriously interfere with the rights of others. It also means that neither the federal government nor any state can encourage or suppress any particular religion. This concept has been referred to as the "wall of separation" between church and state.

The Fourth, Fifth, Sixth, and Eighth Amendments protect persons suspected or accused of crimes. But they also protect the ordinary citizen from intrusion by the police and other government officials. Unreasonable searches and seizures of property are prohibited by the Fourth. Evidence which is obtained from an unlawful search may not be used in a criminal proceeding.

The Fifth Amendment provides that no person shall be required to give evidence which would convict him of a crime; that no one may be deprived of life, liberty, or property without due process of law; and that just compensation be given for property taken for public use, such as a school or highway. The Fifth Amendment stands as a barrier, protecting the people from the arbitrary exercise of governmental power.

The Sixth Amendment assures a speedy and public trial by an impartial jury. It gives a person accused of a crime the right to have subpoenas issued to compel the appearance in court of witnesses in his favor and to be confronted with and cross-examine witnesses against him. The Eighth Amendment prohibits excessive bail or fines and cruel and unusual punishments.

Certainly, the most important of the remaining amendments is the Fourteenth. It grew out of the Civil War and was passed to protect former slaves from oppressive and discriminatory state laws. But its effect has been much broader than that. First, it gives state citizenship to all United States citizens residing in a state. Then, it prohibits states from interfering with the privileges or immunities of American citizens. But the most significant provision is that no state may "deprive any person of life, liberty, or property, without due process of law; nor deny to any person within its jurisdiction the equal protection of the laws." These last provisions apply not only to United States citizens, but to all persons in the state. The Bill of Rights did not protect people from *state* action, but only from *federal* action; but the Fourteenth Amendment has been so interpreted by the U.S. Supreme Court to apply virtually all of the provisions in the Bill of Rights to the states. Thus, the Fourteenth Amendment is one of the most valuable protections that Americans have.

The Bill of Rights was added to the Constitution in 1791. Since then, the Constitution has been amended only sixteen times, and one of these amendments merely repealed another. Most of the others have made only slight changes in the basic law.

THE FEDERAL SYSTEM

The United States government derives all its power from the Constitution. It was understood by the founders that all powers not granted to the United States nor denied to the states were to be retained by the individual states, a concept which is reaffirmed in the Tenth Amendment. This division of powers between the states and the central government is known as the federal system.

The original purpose of a national central government was to perform those tasks that could not efficiently be performed by the states. Such things as dealing with foreign nations, establishing a uniform monetary system, and regulating commerce between the states could better be done by a single national authority. Other governmental responsibilities, such as public school systems, local police and fire protection, and local roads, were left to the states and their subdivisions.

Most of the state governments are quite similar to the national government. Each is headed by an elected executive called a governor. The legislature may be called a general assembly or by some other name, but it generally functions much as Congress does. Almost all of the state legislatures also have two houses. The state court systems generally follow the three-level federal court plan which provides for a trial court, an appellate court, and a supreme court.

States are divided into smaller governmental units, such as cities, towns, villages, and counties. These units have some legislative authority which they receive from the state, and they are responsible for local control within their boundaries.

* * *

Our country is now about 200 years old. Its Constitution has lasted longer than any other nation's. The United States and its Constitution have withstood many crises and criticisms. Since the Constitution was written, this nation has changed from a rural to a highly industrialized society. Still, the "chart" that Daniel Webster mentioned continues to keep the nation securely on course.

The American experiment in democracy has conclusively proved that government "of the people, by the people, for the people" can function effectively for the betterment of its citizens.

EXERCISES

Comprehension. Choose the correct answer.

1. The legislative branch of the American government is called
   (a) the Senate.
   (b) Congress.
   (c) the House of Representatives.
2. The legislative branch of the American government
   (a) enacts laws.
   (b) enforces laws.
   (c) interprets laws.
3. The executive branch of the American government
   (a) enacts laws.
   (b) enforces laws.
   (c) interprets laws.
4. The judicial branch of the American government
   (a) enacts laws.
   (b) enforces laws.
   (c) interprets laws.
5. Freedom of religion, speech, the press, and assembly are protected by the
   (a) Fifth Amendment.
   (b) First Amendment.
   (c) Thirteenth Amendment.
6. The first ten amendments to the Constitution are known as the

(a) Declaration of Independence.
(b) judicial branch.
(c) Bill of Rights.

7. The highest of the federal courts is the
   (a) Court of Appeals.
   (b) Supreme Court.
   (c) Federal court.

8. The most important group of presidential advisers is
   (a) the Senate.
   (b) the Cabinet.
   (c) the House.

9. An individual is protected from having to give evidence which could be used to convict him of a crime by the
   (a) Fifth Amendment.
   (b) First Amendment.
   (c) Articles of Confederation.

10. The division of power between the states and the national central government is known as
   (a) democracy.
   (b) a republic.
   (c) the federal system.

Vocabulary and Usage. Give the meaning of each of the following words. Use each in a sentence.

enact	proportion
enforce	conflict
interpret	dictate
compensation	remarkable
process	virtually

Conversation and Discussion. What is the purpose of dividing the powers of the government into three branches?

XXVII
Choosing the Nation's President

Every four years, Americans participate in a unique and exciting ritual—the selection of the nation's President. The summer before the election, each of the major political parties holds a convention. Delegates from every state meet together to choose candidates for President and Vice-President and to determine the party's program (or *platform*, as it is called).

The number of delegates from each state is determined

by its population and its support for that party in previous elections. The manner of choosing delegates varies from state to state. In some states, delegates are elected by the voters. In others, they are appointed by a state party convention or by state political leaders. Each state also determines whether its delegates will be free to vote as they choose or will be required to vote for the candidate selected at the primary election or state convention.

After routine formalities, convention business usually begins with the creation and acceptance of a party platform. A platform is a very general statement of the party's philosophy, goals, and position on issues of national and international concern. A majority of the convention delegates must vote for the various *planks* of the platform in order for them to be accepted.

The next business of the convention is the nomination of prospective presidential candidates. For each nominee, a lavish nominating speech is made, followed by a long, noisy demonstration with pretty girls waving flags, bands playing, and thousands of people singing, yelling, clapping, and marching with signs.

After all the commotion is over, the delegates get down to the serious work of choosing their party's presidential candidate. His primary qualification is the ability to get elected, but the delegates also consider a nominee's integrity, philosophy, and talent for leadership.

When nominations are completed, votes are taken alphabetically by state. Several roll calls may be necessary before one nominee wins the majority of votes needed to become the party's candidate. In the early balloting, many delegations withhold their support from serious contenders by voting for a prominent politician from their own state, called a *favorite son*. This device makes it possible for state delegations to negotiate with major contenders by agreeing to switch their votes in exchange for some political favor or governmental position. Eventually, enough deals are made so that one man receives a majority of the votes.

Once the presidential candidate is selected, his running mate (the vice-presidential candidate) must be chosen. Usually, the delegates give their presidential candidate the running mate of his choice. Traditionally, a party's presidential and vice-presidential candidates come from different sections of the country and have somewhat different political views. Thus, the party achieves what is called a *balanced ticket*, a combination of candidates that will appeal to many different blocs of voters. After the candidates give their acceptance speeches, the convention is adjourned until the next presidential election four years later.

Actual campaigning for the election traditionally begins on Labor Day. From that time until election day, voters are bombarded from all sides—by radio, television, newspapers, and personal communications—with political material. Sometimes long-standing friendships break up as arguments over issues and candidates rage. Ordinarily soft-spoken people become vehement advocates for their candidate. Neighborhood partisan political workers and precinct captains knock on every door and remind each voter of all that the party has done for him and for the country since the last election.

Each candidate tries to convince a majority of the American voters that he is best qualified to lead the country for the next four years. Since he has only two months in which to do this, a very concentrated campaign is necessary. All the resources of modern communication are used to acquaint voters with the candidates' views and personalities. Television has become a powerful influence, and the candidate who does not have personal appeal via TV is at a great disadvantage. In 1960, a series of television debates between Richard Nixon and John Kennedy probably influenced enough voters to change the course of the election.

Although modern communications have better acquainted voters with candidates and issues, the resulting costs of election campaigns have created a serious problem. The various candidates who participated in the 1972 presidential election raised more than $125 million for their campaigns. Most campaign funds come from private contributions. This, unfortunately, means that the man who gets elected has many "friends" who expect political favors in return for their financial help. Also, the candidates themselves are forced to invest a substantial amount to help pay air fares, hotel bills, and staff salaries while they are on the campaign trail. Banners, automobile stickers, leaflets, pins, and TV and radio time also add up to major expenses. Congress has proposed various ways of easing this situation, either by limiting the amount of money that candidates can spend or by raising campaign funds through taxes and tax incentives.

In 1972, national attention was focused upon presidential politics arising out of an incident commonly known as the *Watergate scandal.* Eight men, including two who were employed by President Nixon's reelection committee, were caught spying in the Democratic National Committee headquarters, located in the Watergate Hotel in Washington, D.C. Although the affair did not substantially influence the election, the Congressional investigation and revelations growing out of it brought the executive branch of government to a virtual standstill for months. Exposed by this incredible scandal were illegal contributions, influence buying, criminal activity, and other sordid conduct by highly regarded administration officials.

When the dust settled and the facts became known, the people discovered that their President had been personally involved in protecting from criminal prosecution those responsible for the Watergate burglary. The people, the press, and Congress were outraged. The Constitutional procedure for removing President Nixon from office (known as impeachment) was put into action. But before the impeachment process was concluded, the President resigned. The United States had demonstrated to the world that in this nation the rule of law applies to everyone; even the President cannot ignore it.

Less than twenty-four hours later, Vice-President Gerald Ford was sworn in as the nation's new President. "The nightmare of Watergate is over," said the new President in his inaugural address. The people collectively sighed in relief and went on with their lives. No shots had been fired; no crisis occurred. The entire process had followed the chart of the Constitution and never strayed off course.

As an additional outgrowth of the "Watergate" scandal, Congress has renewed its efforts to find a way of financing political campaigns with public funds. So far, however, no satisfactory solution has been found.

Because campaigning is extremely expensive and because a candidate must receive a majority of the electoral votes to be elected, presidential politics has, to a large extent, been limited to two major parties—the Democratic and Republican parties. A great number of votes are needed to win a national election. (In 1972, about 64 million Americans voted for presidential candidates.) No candidate can hope to survive by appealing to one or two classes of voters, such as farmers or businessmen. Because of the need for broad appeal, the philosophies of both parties take a middle course so as not to alienate any large blocs of voters. Even so, the Democratic Party is generally supported by workers, farmers, and liberals; the Republicans get most of their support from businessmen, professionals, and the more conservative voters.

Each party has a familiar symbol: for the Democrats it is a donkey, and for the Republicans an elephant. These symbols were created by Thomas Nast, a famous nineteenth-century political cartoonist. The Republican Party is also called the G.O.P. (Grand Old Party).

Although no third-party candidate has ever won a presidential election, third parties have often played an important role by focusing attention upon particular issues and influencing the policies of the two major parties.

To preserve free democratic elections, the rights of all candidates are carefully guarded. They may speak their minds openly, even to the extent of severely criticizing the viewpoints of other candidates, without fear of punishment. This right prevails even when an opponent is an incumbent (currently holding office). The government also protects third parties by prohibiting radio and television stations from giving free publicity to one candidate unless they give equal time to all other candidates.

On the first Tuesday after the first Monday in November, voters cast their ballots for President and Vice-President. Some members of Congress and many state and local officials are also selected at this time. Thanks to voting machines and computers, Americans usually know the winners by late evening.

The President and Vice-President are not actually chosen by popular votes but by *electoral votes*. That is, the people vote for electors who are, as a group, known as the Electoral College. This group selects the President and Vice-President. When a citizen casts his vote for a presidential candidate, he is really choosing electors. Each elector is expected (although not obliged) to vote for the candidate who wins the majority of popular votes in his state.

The number of electors allotted to each state is equal to the total number of representatives and senators who represent that state in Congress. Thus, states with larger populations have more electoral votes. The candidate who receives a majority of the votes in a particular state receives *all* of that state's electoral votes. It is, therefore, possible for a presidential candidate to win a majority of popular votes but not a majority of electoral votes, thereby losing the election. This can happen if his opponent wins by small margins in states with many electoral votes and loses by large margins in states with few electoral votes. At least two presidential elections have been decided this way, most recently in 1888. It is also possible that an elector expected to vote for one candidate will exercise his constitutional right to vote for someone else. However, since electors are prominent members of their respective parties, this rarely happens.

This method of choosing our President has been criticized as archaic and undemocratic, but states with small populations do not want to change it because they have a greater proportional vote in the Electoral College than they would have if the President were chosen by popular vote.

To be elected, candidates for President and Vice-President must receive a majority of the votes in the Electoral College. If no candidate receives a majority, the House of Representatives chooses the President from the top three candidates, and the Senate chooses the Vice-President from the top two candidates having the highest number of electoral votes.

The newly-elected President is inaugurated in January during a solemn, nationally-televised ceremony. He then moves into the White House, appoints members of his Cabinet, and begins the difficult task of trying to persuade Congress to help him fulfill his campaign promises. Since the two major parties are not extremely different, no sudden shift in national policy results from a change in government. Change can be detected only with the passage of time as the new administration becomes accustomed to its powers and responsibilities.

EXERCISES

Comprehension. Choose the correct answer.

1. The President of the United States is elected
   (a) every three years.
   (b) every four years.
   (c) every six years.
2. Each major political party chooses its presidential candidate in a
   (a) delegation.
   (b) convention.
   (c) primary election.
3. A general statement of a party's philosophy, goals, and positions on issues is called a
   (a) platform.
   (b) plank.
   (c) nomination.
4. The traditional symbol of the Democratic Party is
   (a) an elephant.
   (b) a donkey.
   (c) a bear.

5. The traditional symbol of the Republican Party is
   (a) an elephant.
   (b) a donkey.
   (c) a bear.

6. The Democratic Party and the Republican Party are
   (a) not extremely different.
   (b) exactly the same.
   (c) extremely different.

7. Campaigning for the election traditionally begins on
   (a) Easter Sunday.
   (b) Memorial Day.
   (c) Labor Day.

8. The President is actually elected by the
   (a) House of Representatives.
   (b) Electoral College.
   (c) National Convention.

9. The candidate who wins a majority of the popular votes in a state wins
   (a) all the electoral votes of that state.
   (b) some of the electoral votes of that state.
   (c) a proportion of the electoral votes of that state.

10. The election of the President is held on
    (a) the first Monday in May.
    (b) the Fourth of July.
    (c) the first Tuesday after the first Monday in November.

Vocabulary and Usage. Give the meaning of each of the following words. Use each in a sentence.

lavish	vehement
commotion	advocate
qualification	partisan
contender	sordid
bloc	alienate
adjourn	archaic

Conversation and Discussion. Discuss how heads of state are selected and removed in other countries.

XXVIII
Citizenship and its Responsibilities

Every person living in the United States, citizen or not, is entitled to most of our basic freedoms and protections. Still, there are many advantages for people who intend to live here permanently to become citizens. Of these, the most important are the right to remain in the United States and to participate in its government.

With few exceptions, everyone born in the United States is automatically a citizen. An alien who wishes to become a naturalized citizen must fulfill certain legal requirements. He must have been admitted to the United States as a permanent resident. He must have lived in the United States for five years and in the state in which application is made for six months before he can apply for citizenship. He must also be able to read, write, and speak simple English and pass an examination in American history and government. This examination is given at the time the application is filed—after the residency requirements have been fulfilled.

In addition to these requirements, the applicant for citizenship must be of good moral character and be committed to the principles of the United States Constitution. He must also promise to obey the laws of the United States and to renounce allegiance to any foreign country. At the time that an alien files his application, he is required to bring with him two witnesses who know him well, are American citizens, and can testify that his residency requirements have been fulfilled and that he is of good moral character. Next, the Immigration and Naturalization Service investigates to substantiate the truth of the applicant's statements. If the applicant is found eligible, he then comes to court and is sworn in as a United States citizen.

Once a person becomes naturalized, his rights are the same as any native-born citizen, except that he cannot become President or Vice-President of the United States. Along with his rights, the citizen acquires responsibilities toward his country. Some of these responsibilities are shared by residents who are not citizens of the United States.

It is often said that this is a nation of laws, not men. No

individual, no matter how great his rank or wealth, can act in a way prohibited by law. Everyone is equal in the eyes of the law. Obviously, not all laws are perfect. Some are unwise, others unduly burdensome, many are foolish. But they cannot, for any of these reasons, be ignored. The citizen who disapproves of a particular law can legally and peacefully strive for its change through participation in government.

One way that citizens participate in government is by voting. Unfortunately, in every election a sizable percentage of eligible voters never comes to the polls. In 1972, for example, only 46 percent of those eligible voted for a presidential candidate; only 44 percent voted in the congressional election of 1970. When a large number of citizens do not vote, those who do have a greater voice in determining the outcome of the election.

Another way that citizens can participate in government is by communicating with their representatives. In order for an elected official to represent his constituents properly, he must know how they feel about current laws and pending legislation. Do they feel that certain laws are outmoded and should be discarded? Are they for or against a particular bill? A representative who plans to seek reelection is strongly motivated to vote as his constituents desire. But very few voters take the time to write their federal or state representatives and express their views. This creates an opportunity for a small, vocal minority to influence legislation out of proportion to their numbers, and it leads to a distortion of the representative form of government.

Letters are not the only means by which citizens can influence their representatives. Among our basic constitutional guarantees are the rights to assemble peaceably, to petition our government, and to freely express our opinions about the government's policies. However, in expressing dissatisfaction, we must not interfere with the rights of others.

One of the more unpopular civic obligations is the payment of taxes. For most people, the heaviest is the federal income tax. Since 1913, the United States government has been collecting income taxes. As the cost of running the government has gone up, so have tax rates. When the federal income tax was first enacted, people had to pay 1 percent on annual income of less than $20,000. Income in excess of $500,000 was taxed at 7 percent. Today, the income tax rate starts at 14 percent and goes as high as 70 percent for persons earning more than $200,000. These high taxes are necessary to support a federal budget which, in 1974, was $269 billion! This money is put to many uses. In addition to the cost of operating the government itself, there are expenses for defense, education, foreign aid, research, aid to the poor, and countless other services provided by governmental agencies.

Income tax is paid by nearly everyone who earns money in the United States—citizens, alien residents, and visitors. Employers are required to withhold a percentage of their employees' salaries and pay it to the government to be applied toward the employees' tax. Self-employed persons or those earning a substantial amount in addition to their salaries must make quarterly payments on account. By April 15th of every year, each person whose earnings in the previous year exceeded $2050 must file a statement (on forms supplied by the government) listing his earnings, expenses, number of dependents, and other information. After making his calculations on the statement, the taxpayer can determine his tax liability. If he has paid more than his share during the year, he will get a refund; if he has paid less, he must pay the balance.

Federal income tax rates are graduated, which means that persons with larger incomes are taxed at a higher rate than those earning less. An unmarried man earning $6,000 a year would pay about 11 percent of that in taxes. If he earned $10,000, he would pay about 16 percent.

Although the federal government has a substantial amount of information about each taxpayer and penalizes those who file false returns, the income tax law could not be enforced except for the honesty and cooperation of the vast majority of taxpayers.

In addition to federal income taxes, many other taxes are levied by federal, state, and local governments. The funds from these taxes are needed to run various branches of government, such as the courts; to maintain public facilities, such as schools, roads, and parks; and to pay public employees. There are many different kinds of taxes. The most common are those imposed upon income, property, and purchases. The owner of a car, for example, pays several taxes: a sales tax when he buys the car, an annual vehicle tax, and a personal property tax. If he dies while owning the car, his heirs pay an inheritance tax on its value.

Notwithstanding the grumbling one hears about high taxes, Americans know that the taxes they pay make possible the valuable services they receive. Also, when all American taxes are added together, they total only 28 percent of the nation's gross national product. This is the third lowest percentage of all industrial nations.

Another duty of the citizen is to serve on jury duty if selected. A *jury* is a group of people (usually twelve) who are selected tc listen to evidence presented in court. Members of the jury must decide which of the contending parties is right or, in criminal cases, whether the accused has committed a crime. The jury is basic to our system of justice. The right to a jury trial is guaranteed by the U.S. Constitution in Article Three and in the Sixth and Seventh Amendments. This right is also guaranteed by most state constitutions.

Jury panels are generally selected from voter lists. From these panels, which may include several hundred people where courts are busiest, twelve jurors are selected to hear each trial. Many people find jury service an interesting and rewarding experience and look forward to being called again. Jurors usually spend two weeks on duty and are then discharged and a new panel selected.

Every resident of the United States should perform his civic duties in the same spirit that he accepts his lawful rights. Every citizen would do well to remember the inspiring words of President Kennedy: ". . . my fellow Americans: ask not what your country can do for you—ask what you can do for your country."

EXERCISES

Comprehension. Choose the correct answer.

1. One of the most important rights a citizen has is
   (a) to participate in government.
   (b) to pay taxes.
   (c) to serve on a jury.
2. An alien who wishes to become an American citizen must first
   (a) live in the United States for five years.
   (b) become wealthy.
   (c) get a college education.

3. One of the primary responsibilities of a citizen is the responsibility to
   (a) vote.
   (b) attend church.
   (c) exhibit the flag.
4. An immigrant who becomes a naturalized American citizen may not
   (a) vote.
   (b) be elected to Congress.
   (c) be elected President.
5. In 1972, the percentage of eligible voters who actually voted for a presidential candidate was
   (a) 84 percent.
   (b) 62 percent.
   (c) 46 percent.
6. The federal income tax rate that a person pays is determined by
   (a) his wealth.
   (b) his occupation.
   (c) his annual income.
7. A person accused of a crime is entitled to
   (a) peaceable assembly.
   (b) trial by jury.
   (c) service in the armed forces.
8. A basic right in the United States is the right of
   (a) revolution.
   (b) peaceful assembly.
   (c) violence.
9. The purpose of a jury is to
   (a) assess taxes.
   (b) decide the issues in trials.
   (c) grant citizenships.
10. A citizen dissatisfied with the government has the legal right to
    (a) express his views freely.
    (b) overthrow the government.
    (c) increase taxes.

Vocabulary and Usage. Give the meaning of each of the following words. Use each in a sentence.

protection	fulfill
require	eligible
acquire	strive
rank	alien
responsibility	obligation

Conversation and Discussion. Discuss how the responsibilities of citizenship should influence you from day to day.